CHILL CHASER

*Chase away winter chills with this gorgeous afghan.
Worked in worsted weight yarn, the lattice-look design
makes the throw as elegant as it is cuddly.*

Finished Size: 49" x 66"

MATERIALS
Worsted Weight Yarn:
53 ounces,
(1,510 grams, 3,355 yards)
Crochet hook, size H (5.00 mm) **or** size
needed for gauge

GAUGE: Each repeat from point to point =
3³/₄ "; 8 rows = 4"

Gauge Swatch: 7¹/₂ "w x 3"h
Ch 33 **loosely**.
Work same as Afghan Body for 6 rows.
Finish off.

STITCH GUIDE

DECREASE (uses next 4 sc)
YO, insert hook in next sc, YO and pull up a loop, YO and
draw through 2 loops on hook, YO, skip next 2 sc, insert
hook in next sc, YO and pull up a loop, YO and draw through
2 loops on hook, YO and draw through all 3 loops on hook.
ENDING DECREASE (uses last 3 sc)
YO, insert hook in next sc, YO and pull up a loop, YO and
draw through 2 loops on hook, YO, skip next sc, insert hook
in last sc, YO and pull up a loop, YO and draw through
2 loops on hook, YO and draw through all 3 loops on hook.
CLUSTER
Ch 3, YO, insert hook in third ch from hook, YO and pull up
a loop, YO and draw through 2 loops on hook, YO, insert
hook in same ch, YO and pull up a loop, YO and draw
through 2 loops on hook, YO and draw through all 3 loops
on hook *(Figs. 15a & b, page 141)*.

AFGHAN BODY
Ch 209 **loosely**.
Row 1: Sc in second ch from hook and in next 7 chs, ch 2,
★ sc in next 7 chs, skip next 2 chs, sc in next 7 chs, ch 2;
repeat from ★ across to last 8 chs, sc in last 8 chs: 184 sc and
13 ch-2 sps.
Row 2 (Right side): Ch 3, turn; skip first 2 sc, dc in next 6 sc,
(dc, ch 2, dc) in next ch-2 sp, ch 1, (skip next sc, dc in next sc,
ch 1) twice, ★ skip next sc, decrease, dc in next 5 sc, (dc,
ch 2, dc) in next ch-2 sp, ch 1, (skip next sc, dc in next sc,
ch 1) twice; repeat from ★ across to last 4 sc, skip next sc,
work ending decrease; do **not** finish off: 132 sts and 52 sps.

Continued on page 14.

CUDDLY SNOWBALLS

Cozy up with this warm wintertime throw. Strips of popcorn stitches give the look of fluffy snowballs, and herringbone stripes add to the rustic appeal.

Finished Size: 55" x 72"

MATERIALS
Worsted Weight Yarn:
  Blue - 19 ounces, (540 grams, 1,250 yards)
  Ecru - 18 ounces, (510 grams, 1,185 yards)
  Red - 2 ounces, (60 grams, 135 yards)
Crochet hook, size K (6.50 mm) **or** size needed for gauge
Yarn needle

GAUGE: 10 dc and 6 rows = 3¹/₂"

Gauge Swatch: 3¹/₂" square
Ch 12 **loosely**.
Row 1: Dc in fourth ch from hook and in each ch across: 10 sts.
Rows 2-6: Ch 3 **(counts as first dc)**, turn; dc in next dc and in each st across: 10 dc.
Finish off.

Each row is worked across length of Afghan.

STITCH GUIDE

POPCORN
5 Dc in sc indicated, drop loop from hook, insert hook in first dc of 5-dc group, hook dropped loop and draw through *(Fig. 17, page 141)*. Push Popcorn to **right** side.

AFGHAN BODY

With Blue, ch 201 **loosely**.
Row 1 (Right side)**:** Dc in fourth ch from hook and in each ch across: 199 sts.
Note: Loop a short piece of yarn around any stitch to mark Row 1 as **right** side.

Row 2: Ch 3 **(counts as first dc, now and throughout)**, turn; dc in next dc and in each st across: 199 dc.
Row 3: Ch 3, turn; dc in next dc and in each dc across. When changing colors, carry unused color along edge; do **not** cut yarn unless instructed.
Row 4: Ch 3, turn; dc in next dc and in each dc across changing to Ecru in last dc *(Fig. 22a, page 142)*.
Row 5: Ch 3, turn; dc in next dc and in each dc across.
Row 6: Ch 3, turn; dc in next dc and in each dc across changing to Blue in last dc.
Row 7: Ch 1, turn; sc in each dc across.
Row 8: Ch 1, turn; sc in each sc across changing to Ecru in last sc.
Row 9: Ch 1, turn; sc in first 3 sc, (work Popcorn in next sc, sc in next 3 sc) across: 49 Popcorns and 150 sc.
Row 10: Ch 1, turn; sc in first 5 sts, work Popcorn in next sc, (sc in next 3 sts, work Popcorn in next sc) across to last 5 sts, sc in last 5 sts changing to Blue in last sc: 48 Popcorns and 151 sc.
Row 11: Ch 1, turn; sc in each st across: 199 sc.
Row 12: Ch 1, turn; sc in each sc across changing to Ecru in last sc.
Row 13: Ch 3, turn; dc in next sc and in each sc across.
Row 14: Ch 3, turn; dc in next dc and in each dc across changing to Blue in last dc; cut Ecru.
Rows 15-21: Ch 3, turn; dc in next dc and in each dc across.
Row 22: Ch 3, turn; dc in next dc and in each dc across changing to Ecru in last dc.
Repeat Rows 5-22 until Afghan Body measures approximately 53" from beginning ch, ending by working Row 18.
Finish off.

Continued on page 15.

SERENE GRANNY

Shades of purple lend serene beauty to a traditional granny-style afghan.
Dainty flower motifs trim the smaller squares for a pretty touch.

Finished Size: 53" x 73"

MATERIALS
Worsted Weight Yarn:
  Black - 31½ ounces, (890 grams, 2,160 yards)
  Purple - 14½ ounces, (410 grams, 995 yards)
  Lt Purple - 8½ ounces, (240 grams, 580 yards)
  Dk Purple - 2½ ounces, (70 grams, 170 yards)
Crochet hook, size I (5.50 mm) **or** size needed
  for gauge
Yarn needle

GAUGE: Small Square = 2¾"
  Large Square = 5½"

Gauge Swatch: 2¾"
Work same as Small Square.

SMALL SQUARE (Make 206)

Rnd 1 (Right side): With Purple, ch 4, 2 dc in fourth ch from hook, ch 3, (3 dc in same ch, ch 3) 3 times; join with slip st to top of beginning ch-4, finish off: 12 sts and 4 ch-3 sps.
Note: Loop a short piece of yarn around any stitch to mark Rnd 1 as **right** side.
Rnd 2: With **right** side facing, join Black with slip st in any ch-3 sp; ch 3 (**counts as first dc, now and throughout**), (2 dc, ch 3, 3 dc) in same sp, ch 1, ★ (3 dc, ch 3, 3 dc) in next ch-3 sp, ch 1; repeat from ★ 2 times **more**; join with slip st to first dc, finish off: 24 dc and 8 sps.

LARGE SQUARE (Make 72)

Rnd 1 (Right side): With Dk Purple, ch 4, 2 dc in fourth ch from hook, ch 3, (3 dc in same ch, ch 3) 3 times; join with slip st to top of beginning ch-4, finish off: 12 sts and 4 ch-3 sps.
Note: Mark Rnd 1 as **right** side.
Rnd 2: With **right** side facing, join Black with slip st in any ch-3 sp; ch 3, (2 dc, ch 3, 3 dc) in same sp, ch 1, ★ (3 dc, ch 3, 3 dc) in next ch-3 sp, ch 1; repeat from ★ 2 times **more**; join with slip st to first dc, finish off: 24 dc and 8 sps.
Rnd 3: With **right** side facing, join Purple with slip st in any corner ch-3 sp; ch 3, (2 dc, ch 3, 3 dc) in same sp, ch 1, 3 dc in next ch-1 sp, ch 1, ★ (3 dc, ch 3, 3 dc) in next corner ch-3 sp, ch 1, 3 dc in next ch-1 sp, ch 1; repeat from ★ 2 times **more**; join with slip st to first dc, finish off: 36 dc and 12 sps.
Rnd 4: With **right** side facing, join Lt Purple with slip st in any corner ch-3 sp; ch 3, (2 dc, ch 3, 3 dc) in same sp, ch 1, (3 dc in next ch-1 sp, ch 1) twice, ★ (3 dc, ch 3, 3 dc) in next corner ch-3 sp, ch 1, (3 dc in next ch-1 sp, ch 1) twice; repeat from ★ 2 times **more**; join with slip st to first dc, finish off: 48 dc and 16 sps.
Rnd 5: With **right** side facing, join Black with slip st in any corner ch-3 sp; ch 3, (2 dc, ch 3, 3 dc) in same sp, ch 1, (3 dc in next ch-1 sp, ch 1) 3 times, ★ (3 dc, ch 3, 3 dc) in next corner ch-3 sp, ch 1, (3 dc in next ch-1 sp, ch 1) 3 times; repeat from ★ 2 times **more**; join with slip st to first dc, finish off: 60 dc and 20 sps.

Continued on page 15.

BEAUTIFUL BRAIDS

Warm and toasty, this intricate throw gets its rustic look from flecked Aran yarn. Cluster stitches create the braids, and raised front post stitches add texture.

Finished Size: 57½" x 69"

MATERIALS
Worsted Weight Yarn:
    78 ounces, (2,220 grams, 4,525 yards)
Crochet hook, size G (4.00 mm) **or** size needed
    for gauge
Yarn needle

GAUGE: In pattern, 14 sts and 11 rows = 4"
            Each Strip = 9½" wide

Gauge Swatch: 7"w x 4"h
Work same as Strip through Row 11.

STITCH GUIDE

FRONT POST DOUBLE CROCHET
   (abbreviated FPdc)
YO, insert hook from **front** to **back** around post of st indicated, YO and pull up a loop even with loops on hook *(Fig. 11, page 140)*, (YO and draw through 2 loops on hook) twice. Skip sc behind FPdc.

BEGINNING CLUSTER
Ch 2, ★ YO, insert hook in st indicated, YO and pull up a loop even with loops on hook, YO and draw through 2 loops on hook; repeat from ★ once **more**, YO and draw through all 3 loops on hook.

CLUSTER
★ YO, insert hook from **front** to **back** around post of dc indicated **or** in sc indicated *(Fig. 11, page 140)*, YO and pull up a loop even with loops on hook, YO and draw through 2 loops on hook; repeat from ★ 2 times **more**, YO and draw through all 4 loops on hook.

DECREASE
Pull up a loop in next 2 sts, YO and draw through all 3 loops on hook **(counts as one sc)**.

STRIP (Make 6)
Ch 26 **loosely**.
Row 1 (Right side): Dc in fourth ch from hook **(3 skipped chs count as first dc)** and in each ch across: 24 dc.
Note: Loop a short piece of yarn around any stitch to mark Row 1 as **right** side and bottom edge.
Row 2: Ch 1, turn; sc in each dc across.
Row 3: Ch 3 **(counts as first dc, now and throughout)**, turn; dc in next 6 sc, work FPdc around dc one row **below** next sc, dc in next 2 sc, skip next sc, work Cluster around dc one row **below** next sc, skip sc behind Cluster, dc in next 2 sc, work Cluster around dc 2 rows **below** last dc made (to left of first Cluster), skip sc behind Cluster, dc in next 2 sc, work FPdc around dc one row **below** next sc, dc in last 7 sc.
Row 4: Ch 1, turn; sc in each st across.
Row 5: Ch 3, turn; dc in next 6 sc, work FPdc around FPdc one row **below** next sc, dc in next 2 sc, skip next sc, work Cluster around dc one row **below** next sc, skip sc behind Cluster, dc in next 2 sc, work Cluster around dc 2 rows **below** last dc made, skip sc behind Cluster, dc in next 2 sc, work FPdc around FPdc one row **below** next sc, dc in last 7 sc.
Repeat Rows 4 and 5 until Strip measures approximately 66" from beginning ch, ending by working Row 5; do **not** finish off.

BORDER
Rnd 1: Ch 1, do **not** turn; work 195 sc evenly spaced across end of rows; working in free loops of beginning ch *(Fig. 21b, page 142)*, 3 sc in first ch, decrease, sc in next 20 chs, 3 sc in next ch; work 195 sc evenly spaced across end of rows; working across last row, 3 sc in first dc, decrease, sc in each st across to last dc, 3 sc in last dc; join with slip st to first sc: 444 sc.
Rnd 2: Work Beginning Cluster in same st, ch 1, skip next sc, ★ (work Cluster in next sc, ch 1, skip next sc) across to center sc of next corner 3-sc group, (work Cluster, ch 1) 3 times in center sc, skip next sc; repeat from ★ around; join with slip st to top of Beginning Cluster: 230 Clusters and 230 ch-1 sps.
Rnd 3: Ch 1, sc in same st and in each ch-1 sp and each Cluster around working 3 sc in center Cluster of each corner 3-Cluster group; join with slip st to first sc, finish off: 468 sc.

Continued on page 14.

13

BEAUTIFUL BRAIDS Continued from page 12.

ASSEMBLY
Place two Strips with **wrong** sides together and bottom edges at the same end. Working through both loops, whipstitch Strips together **(Fig. 26b, page 143)**, beginning in center sc of first corner 3-sc group and ending in center sc of next corner 3-sc group.
Repeat for remaining Strips.

EDGING
With **right** side facing, join yarn with sc in any sc **(see Joining With Sc, page 142)**; sc evenly around entire Afghan working 3 sc in center sc of each corner 3-sc group; join with slip st to first sc, finish off.

CHILL CHASER Continued from page 6.

Row 3: Ch 1, turn; sc in first st, (sc in next ch-1 sp and in next dc) 3 times, (sc, ch 2, sc) in next ch-2 sp, sc in next dc, work Cluster, skip next dc, sc in next 4 sts, ★ skip next st, (sc in next ch-1 sp and in next dc) 3 times, (sc, ch 2, sc) in next ch-2 sp, sc in next dc, work Cluster, skip next dc, sc in next 4 sts; repeat from ★ across to last dc, skip last dc, sc in next ch: 171 sc, 13 Clusters, and 13 ch-2 sps.
Row 4: Ch 3, turn; skip first 2 sc, dc in next 3 sc, working **behind** next Cluster, tr in skipped dc one row **below** Cluster, dc in next 2 sc, (dc, ch 2, dc) in next ch-2 sp, ch 1, (skip next sc, dc in next sc, ch 1) twice, ★ skip next sc, decrease, dc in next 2 sc, working **behind** next Cluster, tr in skipped dc one row **below** Cluster, dc in next 2 sc, (dc, ch 2, dc) in next ch-2 sp, ch 1, (skip next sc, dc in next sc, ch 1) twice; repeat from ★ across to last 4 sc, skip next sc, work ending decrease: 132 sts and 52 sps.
Repeat Rows 3 and 4 until Afghan Body measures approximately 65" from beginning ch, ending by working Row 4.
Last Row: Ch 1, turn; sc in first st, (sc in next ch-1 sp and in next dc) 3 times, (sc, ch 2, sc) in next ch-2 sp, sc in next 6 sts, ★ skip next st, (sc in next ch-1 sp and in next dc) 3 times, (sc, ch 2, sc) in next ch-2 sp, sc in next 6 sts; repeat from ★ across to last dc, skip last dc, sc in next ch; do **not** finish off: 184 sc and 13 ch-2 sps.

EDGING
Ch 1, turn; slip st in first sc, ch 1, (skip next sc, slip st in next sc, ch 1) 3 times, skip next sc, (slip st, ch 1) twice in next ch-2 sp, ★ (skip next sc, slip st in next sc, ch 1) twice, skip next sc, slip st in next 4 sc, ch 1, (skip next sc, slip st in next sc, ch 1) twice, skip next sc, (slip st, ch 1) twice in next ch-2 sp; repeat from ★ 11 times **more**, (skip next sc, slip st in next sc, ch 1) 3 times, skip next sc, (slip st, ch 1, slip st) in last sc, ch 3; working in end of rows, skip first 2 rows, slip st in next row, (ch 3, skip next row, slip st in next row) across, ch 2; working in ch-2 sps and in free loops of beginning ch **(Fig. 21b, page 142)**, slip st in ch at base of first sc, ch 1, (skip next ch, slip st in next ch, ch 1) twice, skip next ch, slip st in next 4 chs, † ch 1, (skip next ch, slip st in next ch, ch 1) twice, skip next ch, (slip st, ch 1) twice in next ch-2 sp, (skip next ch, slip st in next ch, ch 1) twice, skip next ch, slip st in next 4 chs †; repeat from † to † across to last 6 chs, (ch 1, skip next ch, slip st in next ch) 3 times, ch 2; working in end of rows, slip st in first row, ch 3, (skip next row, slip st in next row, ch 3) across to last 2 rows, skip last 2 rows, slip st in same sc as first slip st, ch 1; join with slip st to first slip st, finish off.

14

CUDDLY SNOWBALLS Continued from page 8.

EDGING

Rnd 1: With **right** side facing, join Ecru with slip st in any st; ch 3, dc evenly around working 3 dc in each corner; join with slip st to first dc.

Rnd 2: Ch 3, dc in next dc and in each dc around working 3 dc in center dc of each corner 3-dc group; join with slip st to first dc, finish off.

HERRINGBONE STITCH

With **right** side facing and Red, work Herringbone Stitch over Rows 5 and 6 *(Fig. 1)*.

Using photo as a guide, work Herringbone Stitch in same manner over all remaining Ecru dc rows.

To work Herringbone Stitch, ★ Bring needle up at A, down at B, up at C, and down at D; repeat from ★ across. Always keep one dc between B and C, and between D and A.

Fig. 1

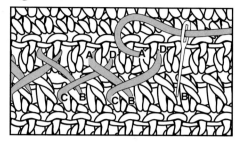

SERENE GRANNY Continued from page 10.

ASSEMBLY

With Black, using Placement Diagram as a guide, and working though both loops, whipstitch Squares together *(Fig. 26b, page 143)*, forming 7 vertical strips of 26 Small Squares **and** 6 vertical strips of 12 Large Squares and 4 Small Squares, beginning in center ch of first corner ch-3 and ending in center ch of next corner ch-3; whipstitch strips together in same manner.

PLACEMENT DIAGRAM

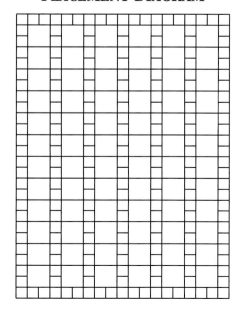

EDGING

Rnd 1: With **right** side facing, join Black with sc in any corner ch-3 sp *(see Joining With Sc, page 142)*; ch 2, sc in same sp, ★ † ch 1, skip next dc, sc in next dc, ch 1, sc in next ch-1 sp, ch 1, skip next dc, sc in next dc, ch 1, [(sc in next sp, ch 1) twice, skip next dc, sc in next dc, ch 1, sc in next ch-1 sp, ch 1, skip next dc, sc in next dc, ch 1] across to next corner ch-3 sp †, (sc, ch 2, sc) in corner ch-3 sp; repeat from ★ 2 times **more**, then repeat from † to † once; join with slip st to first sc: 450 sps.

Rnd 2: Slip st in first corner ch-2 sp, ch 1, (sc, ch 2, sc) in same sp, ch 1, (sc in next ch-1 sp, ch 1) across to next corner ch-2 sp, ★ (sc, ch 2, sc) in corner ch-2 sp, ch 1, (sc in next ch-1 sp, ch 1) across to next corner ch-2 sp; repeat from ★ 2 times **more**; join with slip st to first sc.

Rnd 3: (Slip st, ch 2, slip st) in first corner ch-2 sp, ch 1, (slip st in next ch-1 sp, ch 1) across to next corner ch-2 sp, ★ (slip st, ch 2, slip st) in corner ch-2 sp, ch 1, (slip st in next ch-1 sp, ch 1) across to next corner ch-2 sp; repeat from ★ 2 times **more**; join with slip st to first slip st, finish off.

BED OF ROSES

As beautiful as a bed of roses in full bloom, this delicate throw works up in no time using long double crochets for a teardrop effect. Flowing fringe lends stylish flair.

Finished Size: 47" x 66¹/₂"

MATERIALS
Worsted Weight Yarn:
Rose - 27¹/₂ ounces,
(780 grams, 1,330 yards)
Dk Rose - 20 ounces,
(570 grams, 965 yards)
Ecru - 20 ounces,
(570 grams, 965 yards)
Crochet hook, size H (5.00 mm) **or** size needed for gauge

GAUGE: In pattern, 3 repeats = 3¹/₂ ";
11 rows = 4¹/₂ "

Gauge Swatch: 4³/₄ "w x 4¹/₂ "h
Ch 20 **loosely**.
Work same as Afghan for 11 rows.

STITCH GUIDE

> **LONG DOUBLE CROCHET (abbreviated LDC)**
> YO, working **around** same ch, insert hook in center st of 3-st group one row **below**, YO and pull up a loop even with last dc made, (YO and draw through 2 loops on hook) twice **(Fig. 9, page 140)**.

AFGHAN

With Rose, ch 168 **loosely**.
Row 1 (Right side)**:** Hdc in third ch from hook **(2 skipped chs count as first hdc)**, ★ ch 1, skip next 3 chs, 3 dc in next ch; repeat from ★ across to last 5 chs, ch 1, skip next 3 chs, hdc in last 2 chs; finish off: 124 sts and 41 ch-1 sps.
Note: Loop a short piece of yarn around any stitch to mark Row 1 as **right** side.
Row 2: With **wrong** side facing, join Dk Rose with slip st in first hdc; ch 2 **(counts as first hdc, now and throughout)**, 3 dc in next ch-1 sp, (ch 1, 3 dc in next ch-1 sp) across to last 2 hdc, skip next hdc, hdc in last hdc; finish off: 125 sts and 40 ch-1 sps.
Row 3: With **right** side facing, join Ecru with slip st in first hdc; ch 2, hdc in same st, ch 1, ★ dc in next ch-1 sp, work LDC, dc in same ch-1 sp as last dc made, ch 1; repeat from ★ across to last 4 sts, skip next 3 sts, 2 hdc in last hdc; finish off: 124 sts and 41 ch-1 sps.
Row 4: With **wrong** side facing, join Rose with slip st in first hdc; ch 2, dc in next ch-1 sp, work LDC, dc in same sp as last dc made, ★ ch 1, dc in next ch-1 sp, work LDC, dc in same sp as last dc made; repeat from ★ across to last 2 hdc, skip next hdc, hdc in last hdc; finish off: 125 sts and 40 ch-1 sps.
Row 5: With Dk Rose, repeat Row 3.
Row 6: With Ecru, repeat Row 4.
Row 7: With Rose, repeat Row 3.
Row 8: With Dk Rose, repeat Row 4.
Repeat Rows 3-8 until Afghan measures approximately 66¹/₂ " from beginning ch, ending by working Row 7.

Holding 7 strands of Rose together, each 22" long, add fringe in sps across short edges of Afghan **(Figs. 27a & c, page 143)**.

CUDDLY VALENTINE

Lacy and elegant, this delicate throw is as easy to stitch as it is beautiful.
Rows of filet hearts make it a fitting "valentine" for a special friend.

Finished Size: 46" x 61"

MATERIALS

100% Cotton Worsted Weight Yarn:
43 ounces, (1,220 grams, 2,030 yards)
Crochet hook, size F (3.75 mm) **or** size needed
for gauge

GAUGE: 16 dc and 8 rows = 4"

Gauge Swatch: 4" square
Ch 18 **loosely.**
Row 1: Dc in fourth ch from hook and in each ch across:
16 sts.
Rows 2-8: Ch 3 **(counts as first dc)**, turn; dc in next dc and
in each st across.
Finish off.

Each row is worked across length of Afghan.

STITCH GUIDE

ADD ON DOUBLE CROCHET
YO, insert hook into base of last dc **(Fig. 1)**, YO and
pull up a loop, YO and draw through one loop on hook,
(YO and draw through 2 loops on hook) twice.

Fig. 1

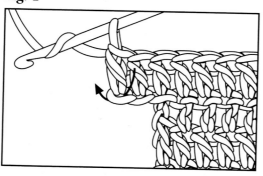

AFGHAN

Ch 213 **loosely.**
Row 1 (Right side): Dc in fourth ch from hook and in each ch
across: 211 sts.
Row 2: Ch 5, turn; dc in fourth ch from hook and in next ch, dc
in next dc, (ch 2, skip next 2 dc, dc in next st) across, add on
3 dc: 217 sts.
Row 3: Ch 5, turn; dc in fourth ch from hook and in next ch, dc
in next dc, ch 2, skip next 2 dc, dc in next dc, ch 2, dc in next
dc, 2 dc in next ch-2 sp, ★ dc in next dc, (ch 2, dc in next dc) 5
times, 2 dc in next ch-2 sp; repeat from ★ 10 times **more**, (dc
in next dc, ch 2) 3 times, skip next 2 dc, dc in next st, add on
3 dc: 223 sts.
Row 4: Ch 5, turn; dc in fourth ch from hook and in next ch, dc
in next dc, ch 2, skip next 2 dc, dc in next dc, (ch 2, dc in next
dc) twice, 2 dc in next ch-2 sp, dc in next 4 dc, 2 dc in next
ch-2 sp, ★ dc in next dc, (ch 2, dc in next dc) 3 times, 2 dc in
next ch-2 sp, dc in next 4 dc, 2 dc in next ch-2 sp; repeat from
★ 10 times **more**, (dc in next dc, ch 2) twice, skip next 2 dc,
dc in next st, add on 3 dc: 229 sts.
Row 5: Ch 5, turn; dc in fourth ch from hook and in next ch, dc
in next dc, ch 2, skip next 2 dc, ★ (dc in next dc, ch 2) twice,
dc in next 10 dc, 2 dc in next ch-2 sp; repeat from ★ 11 times
more, (dc in next dc, ch 2) 3 times, skip next 2 dc, dc in next
st, add on 3 dc: 235 sts.
Row 6: Ch 5, turn; dc in fourth ch from hook and in next ch, dc
in next dc, ch 2, skip next 2 dc, dc in next dc, (ch 2, dc in next
dc) twice, 2 dc in next ch-2 sp, dc in next 10 dc, ch 2, ★ skip
next 2 dc, dc in next dc, ch 2, dc in next dc, 2 dc in next
ch-2 sp, dc in next 10 dc, ch 2; repeat from ★ 10 times **more**,
skip next 2 dc, (dc in next dc, ch 2) 4 times, skip next 2 dc, dc
in next st, add on 3 dc: 241 sts.
Row 7: Turn; slip st in first 4 sts, ch 3, 2 dc in next ch-2 sp, dc
in next dc, (ch 2, dc in next dc) 3 times, 2 dc in next ch-2 sp,
dc in next 10 dc, ch 2, skip next 2 dc, dc in next dc, ★ ch 2,
dc in next dc, 2 dc in next ch-2 sp, dc in next 10 dc, ch 2, skip next
2 dc, dc in next dc; repeat from ★ 10 times **more**, (ch 2, dc in
next dc) twice, 2 dc in next ch-2 sp, dc in next dc, leave
remaining 3 sts unworked; do **not** finish off: 235 sts.

Continued on page 25.

HEARTS & LACE

You'll love snuggling up with an afghan featuring soft heart motifs and scalloped trim!
We chose blue and ecru yarns, but you can use any colors to match your decor.

Finished Size: 44" x 67"

MATERIALS

Worsted Weight Yarn:
  Blue - 20¾ ounces, (590 grams, 1,425 yards)
  Ecru - 17½ ounces, (500 grams, 1,200 yards)
  Crochet hook, size H (5.00 mm) **or** size needed
    for gauge

GAUGE: Each Square = 8"

Gauge Swatch: 5¼ "
Work same as First Square through Rnd 4.

STITCH GUIDE

2-DC CLUSTER
Ch 3, YO, insert hook in third ch from hook, YO and pull up
a loop, YO and draw through 2 loops on hook, YO, insert
hook in same ch, YO and pull up a loop, YO and draw
through 2 loops on hook, YO and draw through all 3 loops
on hook *(Figs. 15a & b, page 141)*.
BEGINNING 3-DC CLUSTER (uses one st or sp)
Ch 2, ★ YO, insert hook in st or sp indicated, YO and pull up
a loop, YO and draw through 2 loops on hook; repeat from ★
once **more**, YO and draw through all 3 loops on hook.
3-DC CLUSTER (uses one st or sp)
★ YO, insert hook in st or sp indicated, YO and pull up a
loop, YO and draw through 2 loops on hook; repeat from ★
2 times **more**, YO and draw through all 4 loops on hook.

For markers indicated on Rnd 6, 2 different colors are
recommended, using the same color for each type of joining
specified. Remove markers when no longer needed.

FIRST VERTICAL STRIP
FIRST SQUARE

With Blue, ch 4; join with slip st to form a ring.
Rnd 1 (Right side): Ch 1, 8 sc in ring; join with slip st to
first sc.
Note: Loop a short piece of yarn around any stitch to mark
Rnd 1 as **right** side.

Rnd 2: Work 2-dc Cluster, in next sc work [tr, 2-dc Cluster, dtr,
2-dc Cluster, tr], work 2-dc Cluster, dc in next sc, work 2-dc
Cluster, sc in next sc, work 2-dc Cluster, dtr in next sc, work
2-dc Cluster, sc in next sc, work 2-dc Cluster, dc in next sc,
work 2-dc Cluster, in next sc work [tr, 2-dc Cluster, dtr, place
marker around dtr just made for st placement, 2-dc Cluster, tr],
work 2-dc Cluster; join with slip st to same st as joining,
finish off: 12 2-dc Clusters and 11 sts.
Rnd 3: With **right** side facing and working in Back Loops Only
(Fig. 20, page 142), join Ecru with slip st in marked dtr; ch 4
(counts as first hdc plus ch 2), (hdc in same st, ch 2) twice,
skip next Cluster, dc in next tr, ch 2, skip next 2 Clusters, dc in
next tr, ch 2, skip next Cluster, (hdc, ch 2) 3 times in next dtr,
skip next Cluster, sc in next tr, ch 2, skip next Cluster, dc in next
dc, ch 2, skip next Cluster, (dtr, ch 2) 3 times in next sc, skip
next Cluster, (hdc, ch 2) twice in next dtr, skip next Cluster, (dtr,
ch 2) 3 times in next sc, skip next Cluster, dc in next dc, ch 2,
skip next Cluster, sc in next tr, ch 2, skip next Cluster; join with
slip st to first hdc: 20 sts and 20 ch-2 sps.
Rnd 4: Ch 3 **(counts as first dc)**, working in Back Loops
Only, dc in next 2 chs, 3 dc in next hdc, [dc in next 2 chs, (dc in
next st and in next 2 chs) 4 times, 3 dc in next st] twice, place
marker in center dc of 3-dc group just made for st placement,
dc in next 2 chs, (dc in next st and in next 2 chs) 4 times, 3 dc
in next st, dc in next 2 chs, (dc in next st and in next 2 chs) 3
times; join with slip st to first dc, finish off: 68 dc.
Rnd 5: With **right** side facing and working in Back Loops Only,
join Blue with slip st in marked dc; work (Beginning 3-dc
Cluster, ch 3, 3-dc Cluster) in same st, ★ † skip next 3 dc, work
(3-dc Cluster, ch 3, 3-dc Cluster) in next dc, [skip next 2 dc,
work (3-dc Cluster, ch 3, 3-dc Cluster) in next dc] 3 times, skip
next 3 dc †, work [3-dc Cluster, (ch 3, 3-dc Cluster) twice] in
next dc; repeat from ★ 2 times **more**, then repeat from † to †
once, work 3-dc Cluster in same st as Beginning 3-dc Cluster,
ch 3; join with slip st to **both** loops at top of Beginning 3-dc
Cluster, finish off: 44 3-dc Clusters.

Continued on page 26.

COUNTRY HEARTS

Dimensional hearts and traditional granny squares make this adorable afghan perfect for a country home. The wrap is worked in squares and then assembled, so it's a great "traveling" project.

Finished Size: 55" x 68"

MATERIALS

Worsted Weight Yarn:
  Ecru - 18 ounces, (510 grams, 1,235 yards)
  Green - 12 ounces, (340 grams, 820 yards)
  Rose - 12 ounces, (340 grams, 820 yards)
  Lt Rose - 11 ounces, (310 grams, 755 yards)
Crochet hook, size I (5.50 mm) **or** size needed
  for gauge
Yarn needle

GAUGE: Each Square = 6³/₄"

Gauge Swatch: 4¹/₂ "
Work same as Square A through Rnd 5.

STITCH GUIDE

PICOT
Ch 3, dc in third ch from hook.

	Square A Make 12	Square B Make 20	Square C Make 15	Square D Make 16
Rnd 1	Lt Rose	Rose	Green	Green
Rnd 2	Lt Rose	Rose	Lt Rose	Rose
Rnd 3	Lt Rose	Rose	Rose	Lt Rose
Rnd 4	Rose	Lt Rose	Green	Green
Rnd 5	Rose	Lt Rose	Lt Rose	Rose
Rnd 6	Green	Green	Ecru	Ecru
Rnd 7	Ecru	Ecru	--	--

SQUARES A & B

With color indicated for Rnd 1, ch 8 **loosely**.

Rnd 1 (Right side): 3 Tr in fourth ch from hook, tr in next ch, dc in next ch, hdc in next ch, 3 sc in last ch; working in free loops of beginning ch *(Fig. 21b, page 142)*, hdc in next ch, dc in next ch, tr in next ch, (3 tr, ch 3, slip st) in same ch as first tr; do **not** join: 16 sts and 2 ch-3 sps.

Note: Loop a short piece of yarn around any stitch to mark Rnd 1 as **right** side.

Rnd 2: Ch 1, sc in same ch as last slip st made, ch 1, dc in next ch-3 sp, ch 1, place marker around ch-1 just made for st placement, (tr, ch 1) 4 times in next tr, tr in next tr, ch 1, skip next tr, (dc in next st, ch 1, skip next st) twice, (dc, ch 4, dc) in next sc, ch 1, skip next sc, (dc in next st, ch 1, skip next st) twice, tr in next tr, ch 1, (tr, ch 1) 4 times in next tr, dc in last ch-3 sp, ch 1; join with slip st to first sc: 19 sts and 19 sps.

Rnd 3: Ch 1, **turn**; skip first ch-1 sp, slip st in next dc, work Picot, (skip next ch-1 sp, slip st in next st, work Picot) 7 times, skip next dc, (slip st, work Picot) twice in next ch-4 sp, skip next dc, slip st in next dc, (work Picot, skip next ch-1 sp, slip st in next st) 7 times, ch 1; join with slip st in same st as previous joining, finish off: 17 Picots.

Rnd 4: With **wrong** side facing and working in **front** of Picot, join next color with sc in marked ch-1 sp on Rnd 2 *(see Joining With Sc, page 142)*; remove marker, ch 6, working in **front** of next Picot, sc in ch-1 sp one rnd **below** Picot, ch 4 **(counts as first dc plus ch 1)**, **turn**; (3 dc, ch 3, 3 dc) in next ch-6 sp, ch 1, dc in next sc, ch 1, working **behind** Picots and in skipped ch-1 sps on Rnd 2, (sc in next sp, ch 1) twice, (dc, ch 3, dc) in next sp, ch 1, hdc in next sp, ch 1, sc in next sp, (ch 1, slip st in next sp) twice, ch 2, skip next slip st, (slip st, ch 2) twice in sp **before** next slip st, (slip st in next sp, ch 1) twice, sc in next sp, ch 1, hdc in next sp, ch 1, (dc, ch 3, dc) in next sp, ch 1, (sc in next sp, ch 1) twice; join with slip st to first dc, do **not** finish off: 26 sts and 22 sps along outer edge.

Continued on page 24.

Rnd 5: Slip st in first ch-1 sp, ch 3 **(counts as first dc, now and throughout)**, do **not** turn; 2 dc in same sp, ch 1, (3 dc, ch 3, 3 dc) in next ch-3 sp, ch 1, (3 dc in next ch-1 sp, ch 1, skip next ch-1 sp) twice, (3 dc, ch 3, 3 dc) in next ch-3 sp, ch 1, (skip next ch-1 sp, 3 dc in next ch-1 sp, ch 1) twice, skip next ch-2 sp, 2 dc in next slip st, (dc, ch 3, dc) in next ch-2 sp, 2 dc in next slip st, ch 1, skip next ch-2 sp, (3 dc in next ch-1 sp, ch 1, skip next ch-1 sp) twice, (3 dc, ch 3, 3 dc) in next ch-3 sp, ch 1, skip next ch-1 sp, 3 dc in next ch-1 sp, ch 1, skip last ch-1 sp; join with slip st to first dc, finish off: 48 dc and 16 sps.

Rnds 6 and 7: With **right** side facing, join next color with slip st in any corner ch-3 sp; ch 3, (2 dc, ch 3, 3 dc) in same sp, ch 1, (3 dc in next ch-1 sp, ch 1) across to next corner ch-3 sp, ★ (3 dc, ch 3, 3 dc) in corner ch-3 sp, ch 1, (3 dc in next ch-1 sp, ch 1) across to next corner ch-3 sp; repeat from ★ 2 times **more**; join with slip st to first dc, finish off: 72 dc and 24 sps.

SQUARES C & D

Referring to table, page 22, make the number of Squares specified in the colors indicated.

Rnd 1 (Right side)**:** With Green, ch 4, 2 dc in fourth ch from hook **(3 skipped chs count as first dc)**, ch 3, (3 dc in same ch, ch 3) 3 times; join with slip st to first dc, finish off: 12 dc and 4 ch-3 sps.
Note: Mark Rnd 1 as **right** side.
Rnd 2: With **right** side facing, join next color with slip st in any ch-3 sp; ch 3, (2 dc, ch 3, 3 dc) in same sp, ch 1, ★ (3 dc, ch 3, 3 dc) in next ch-3 sp, ch 1; repeat from ★ 2 times **more**; join with slip st to first dc, finish off: 24 dc and 8 sps.
Rnd 3: With **right** side facing, join next color with slip st in any corner ch-3 sp; ch 3, (2 dc, ch 3, 3 dc) in same sp, ch 1, 3 dc in next ch-1 sp, ch 1, ★ (3 dc, ch 3, 3 dc) in next corner ch-3 sp, ch 1, 3 dc in next ch-1 sp, ch 1; repeat from ★ 2 times **more**; join with slip st to first dc, finish off: 36 dc and 12 sps.

Rnds 4-6: With **right** side facing, join next color with slip st in any corner ch-3 sp; ch 3, (2 dc, ch 3, 3 dc) in same sp, ch 1, (3 dc in next ch-1 sp, ch 1) across to next corner ch-3 sp, ★ (3 dc, ch 3, 3 dc) in corner ch-3 sp, ch 1, (3 dc in next ch-1 sp, ch 1) across to next corner ch-3 sp; repeat from ★ 2 times **more**; join with slip st to first dc, finish off: 72 dc and 24 sps.

ASSEMBLY

With Ecru, using Placement Diagram as a guide, and working though both loops, whipstitch Squares together *(Fig. 26b, page 143)*, forming 7 vertical strips of 9 Squares each, beginning in center ch of first corner ch-3 and ending in center ch of next corner ch-3; whipstitch strips together in same manner.

PLACEMENT DIAGRAM

B	C	B	C	B	C	B
D	A	D	A	D	A	D
B	C	B	C	B	C	B
D	A	D	A	D	A	D
B	C	B	C	B	C	B
D	A	D	A	D	A	D
B	C	B	C	B	C	B
D	A	D	A	D	A	D
B	C	B	C	B	C	B

EDGING

Rnd 1: With **right** side facing, join Ecru with sc in any corner ch-3 sp; ch 2, sc in same sp, ★ † ch 1, skip next dc, sc in next dc, ch 1, (sc in next ch-1 sp, ch 1, skip next dc, sc in next dc, ch 1) 5 times, [(sc in next sp, ch 1) twice, skip next dc, sc in next dc, ch 1, (sc in next ch-1 sp, ch 1, skip next dc, sc in next dc, ch 1) 5 times] across to next corner ch-3 sp †, (sc, ch 2, sc) in corner ch-3 sp; repeat from ★ 2 times **more**, then repeat from † to † once; join with slip st to first sc: 416 sps.

Rnd 2: Slip st in first corner ch-2 sp, ch 1, (sc, ch 2, sc) in same sp, ch 1, (sc in next ch-1 sp, ch 1) across to next corner ch-2 sp, ★ (sc, ch 2, sc) in corner ch-2 sp, ch 1, (sc in next ch-1 sp, ch 1) across to next corner ch-2 sp; repeat from ★ 2 times **more**; join with slip st to first sc, finish off: 420 sps.

Rnd 3: With **right** side facing, join Green with slip st in any corner ch-2 sp; ch 3, (2 dc, ch 3, 3 dc) in same sp, ch 1, skip next ch-1 sp, (3 dc in next ch-1 sp, ch 1, skip next ch-1 sp) across to next corner ch-2 sp, ★ (3 dc, ch 3, 3 dc) in corner ch-2 sp, ch 1, skip next ch-1 sp, (3 dc in next ch-1 sp, ch 1, skip next ch-1 sp) across to next corner ch-2 sp; repeat from ★ 2 times **more**; join with slip st to first dc, finish off: 214 sps.

Rnd 4: With **right** side facing, join Rose with slip st in any corner ch-3 sp; ch 3, (2 dc, ch 3, 3 dc) in same sp, ch 1, (3 dc in next ch-1 sp, ch 1) across to next corner ch-3 sp, ★ (3 dc, ch 3, 3 dc) in corner ch-3 sp, ch 1, (3 dc in next ch-1 sp, ch 1) across to next corner ch-3 sp; repeat from ★ 2 times **more**; join with slip st to first dc, finish off: 218 sps.

Rnd 5: With Lt Rose, repeat Rnd 4: 222 sps.

Rnd 6: With Green, repeat Rnd 4: 226 sps.

Rnd 7: With **right** side facing, join Ecru with slip st in any corner ch-3 sp; ch 3, (2 dc, ch 3, 3 dc) in same sp, ch 1, (3 dc in next ch-1 sp, ch 1) across to next corner ch-3 sp, ★ (3 dc, ch 3, 3 dc) in corner ch-3 sp, ch 1, (3 dc in next ch-1 sp, ch 1) across to next corner ch-3 sp; repeat from ★ 2 times **more**; join with slip st to first dc, do **not** finish off: 690 dc and 230 sps.

Rnd 8: Slip st in next dc, ch 1, sc in same st, ch 1, (sc, ch 2, sc) in next corner ch-3 sp, ★ ch 1, skip next dc, sc in next dc, ch 1, (sc in next ch-1 sp, ch 1, skip next dc, sc in next dc, ch 1) across to next corner ch-3 sp, (sc, ch 2, sc) in corner ch-3 sp; repeat from ★ 2 times **more**, ch 1, (skip next dc, sc in next dc, ch 1, sc in next ch-1 sp, ch 1) across; join with slip st to first sc: 464 sps.

Rnd 9: Slip st in first ch-1 sp, ch 2, (slip st, ch 3, slip st) in next corner ch-2 sp, ch 2, ★ (slip st in next ch-1 sp, ch 2) across to next corner ch-2 sp, (slip st, ch 3, slip st) in corner ch-2 sp, ch 2; repeat from ★ 2 times **more**, (slip st in next ch-1 sp, ch 2) across; join with slip st to first slip st, finish off.

CUDDLY VALENTINE Continued from page 18.

Row 8: Turn; slip st in first 4 sts, ch 3, 2 dc in next ch-2 sp, dc in next dc, (ch 2, dc in next dc) twice, ★ ch 2, skip next 2 dc, dc in next 10 dc, (ch 2, dc in next dc) twice; repeat from ★ 11 times **more**, 2 dc in next ch-2 sp, dc in next dc, leave remaining 3 sts unworked: 229 sts.

Row 9: Turn; slip st in first 4 sts, ch 3, 2 dc in next ch-2 sp, dc in next dc, ch 2, dc in next dc, ch 2, skip next 2 dc, dc in next 4 dc, ch 2, skip next 2 dc, dc in next dc, ★ (ch 2, dc in next dc) 3 times, ch 2, skip next 2 dc, dc in next 4 dc, ch 2, skip next 2 dc, dc in next dc; repeat from ★ 10 times **more**, (ch 2, dc in next dc) twice, 2 dc in next ch-2 sp, dc in next dc, leave remaining 3 sts unworked: 223 sts.

Row 10: Turn; slip st in first 4 sts, ch 3, 2 dc in next ch-2 sp, dc in next dc, (ch 2, dc in next dc) twice, ch 2, skip next 2 dc, dc in next dc, ★ (ch 2, dc in next dc) 5 times, ch 2, skip next 2 dc, dc in next dc; repeat from ★ 10 times **more**, ch 2, dc in next dc, 2 dc in next ch-2 sp, dc in next dc, leave remaining 3 sts unworked: 217 sts.

Row 11: Turn; slip st in first 4 sts, ch 3, (2 dc in next ch-2 sp, dc in next dc) across to last 3 sts, leave remaining sts unworked: 211 sts.

Rows 12-91: Repeat Rows 2-11, 8 times. Finish off.

Rnd 6: With **right** side facing, join Ecru with sc in same st as joining *(see Joining With Sc, page 142)*; ch 5, sc in same st, † (dc, ch 3, dc) in next ch-3 sp, [skip next Cluster, sc in sp **before** next Cluster, (dc, ch 3, dc) in next ch-3 sp] 5 times *(Fig. 23, page 143)*, (sc, ch 5, sc) in next Cluster †, place marker around last ch-5 made for next Square joining, repeat from † to † once, place marker around last ch-5 made for next Strip joining, repeat from † to † once, (dc, ch 3, dc) in next ch-3 sp, [skip next Cluster, sc in sp **before** next Cluster, (dc, ch 3, dc) in next ch-3 sp] 5 times; join with slip st to first sc, finish off: 28 sps.

NEXT 7 SQUARES

Work same as First Square through Rnd 5: 44 Clusters.

Rnd 6 (Joining rnd)**:** With **right** side facing, join Ecru with sc in same st as joining; ch 5, sc in same st, † (dc, ch 3, dc) in next ch-3 sp, [skip next Cluster, sc in sp **before** next Cluster, (dc, ch 3, dc) in next ch-3 sp] 5 times †, (sc, ch 5, sc) in next Cluster, place marker around last ch-5 made for next Square joining, repeat from † to † once, sc in next Cluster, ch 2, holding Squares with **wrong** sides together, slip st in ch-5 sp marked for next Square joining on **adjacent Square** *(Fig. 24, page 143)*, ch 2, sc in same st as last sc on **new Square**, dc in next ch-3 sp, ch 1, slip st in next ch-3 sp on **adjacent Square**, ch 1, dc in same sp on **new Square**, ★ skip next Cluster, sc in sp **before** next Cluster, dc in next ch-3 sp, ch 1, slip st in next ch-3 sp on **adjacent Square**, ch 1, dc in same sp on **new Square**; repeat from ★ 4 times **more**, sc in next Cluster, ch 2, slip st in next corner ch-5 sp on **adjacent Square**, ch 2, sc in same st as last sc on **new Square**, repeat from † to † once; join with slip st to first sc, finish off.

REMAINING 4 STRIPS
FIRST SQUARE

Work same as First Square of First Vertical Strip through Rnd 5: 44 Clusters.

Rnd 6 (Joining rnd)**:** With **right** side facing, join Ecru with sc in same st as joining; † (dc, ch 3, dc) in next ch-3 sp, [skip next Cluster, sc in sp **before** next Cluster, (dc, ch 3, dc) in next ch-3 sp] 5 times, (sc, ch 5, sc) in next Cluster †, place marker around last ch-5 made for next Square joining, repeat from † to † once, place marker around last ch-5 made for next Strip joining, (dc, ch 3, dc) in next ch-3 sp, [skip next Cluster, sc in sp **before** next Cluster, (dc, ch 3, dc) in next ch-3 sp] 5 times, sc in next Cluster, ch 2, holding Squares with **wrong** sides together, slip st in ch-5 sp marked for next Strip joining on **adjacent Strip**, ch 2, sc in same st as last sc on **new Square**, dc in next ch-3 sp, ch 1, slip st in next ch-3 sp on **adjacent Square**, ch 1, dc in same sp on **new Square**, ★ skip next Cluster, sc in sp **before** next Cluster, dc in next ch-3 sp, ch 1, slip st in next ch-3 sp on **adjacent Square**, ch 1, dc in same sp on **new Square**; repeat from ★ 4 times **more**, sc in same st as first sc, ch 2, slip st in next joining slip st on **adjacent Square**, ch 2; join with slip st to first sc on **new Square**, finish off.

NEXT 6 SQUARES

Work same as First Square of First Vertical Strip through Rnd 5: 44 Clusters.

Rnd 6 (Joining rnd)**:** With **right** side facing, join Ecru with sc in same st as joining; † (dc, ch 3, dc) in next ch-3 sp, [skip next Cluster, sc in sp **before** next Cluster, (dc, ch 3, dc) in next ch-3 sp] 5 times †, (sc, ch 5, sc) in next Cluster, place marker around last ch-5 made for next Square joining, repeat from † to † once, sc in next Cluster, ch 2, holding Squares with **wrong** sides together, slip st in ch-5 sp marked for next Square joining on **adjacent Square**, ♥ ch 2, sc in same st as last sc on **new Square**, dc in next ch-3 sp, ch 1, slip st in next ch-3 sp on **adjacent Square**, ch 1, dc in same sp on **new Square**, ★ skip next Cluster, sc in sp **before** next Cluster, dc in next ch-3 sp, ch 1, slip st in next ch-3 sp on **adjacent Square**, ch 1, dc in same sp on **new Square**; repeat from ★ 4 times **more** ♥, sc in next Cluster, ch 2, slip st in next joining slip st on **adjacent Square**, repeat from ♥ to ♥ once, sc in same st as first sc, ch 2, slip st in next joining slip st on **adjacent Square**, ch 2; join with slip st to first sc on **new Square**, finish off.

LAST SQUARE

Work same as First Square of First Vertical Strip through Rnd 5: 44 Clusters.

Rnd 6 (Joining rnd)**:** With **right** side facing, join Ecru with sc in same st as joining; † (dc, ch 3, dc) in next ch-3 sp, [skip next Cluster, sc in sp **before** next Cluster, (dc, ch 3, dc) in next ch-3 sp] 5 times †, (sc, ch 5, sc) in next Cluster, place marker around last ch-5 made for next Square joining, repeat from † to † once, sc in next Cluster, ch 2, holding Squares with **wrong** sides together, slip st in ch-5 sp marked for next Square joining on **adjacent Square**, ♥ ch 2, sc in same st as last sc on **new Square**, dc in next ch-3 sp, ch 1, slip st in next ch-3 sp on **adjacent Square**, ch 1, dc in same sp on **new Square**, ★ skip next Cluster, sc in sp **before** next Cluster, dc in next ch-3 sp, ch 1, slip st in next ch-3 sp on **adjacent Square**, ch 1, dc in same sp on **new Square**; repeat from ★ 4 times **more** ♥, sc in next Cluster, ch 2, slip st in next joining slip st on **adjacent Square**, repeat from ♥ to ♥ once, sc in same st as first sc, ch 2, slip st in ch-5 sp marked for next Square joining on **adjacent Square**, ch 2; join with slip st to first sc on **new Square**, finish off.

EDGING

Rnd 1: With **right** side facing, join Ecru with sc in any corner ch-5 sp; ch 5, sc in same sp, ch 5, ★ (sc in next sp, ch 5) across to next corner ch-5 sp, (sc, ch 5) twice in corner sp; repeat from ★ 2 times **more**, (sc in next sp, ch 5) across; join with slip st to first sc, finish off: 208 ch-5 sps.

Rnd 2: With **right** side facing, join Blue with slip st in any corner ch-5 sp; work Beginning 3-dc Cluster in same sp, ★ † (work 2-dc Cluster, work 3-dc Cluster in same sp) twice, (work 3-dc Cluster in next ch-5 sp, work 2-dc Cluster, work 3-dc Cluster in same sp) across to next corner ch-5 sp †, work 3-dc Cluster in corner ch-5 sp; repeat from ★ 2 times **more**, then repeat from † to † once; join with slip st to top of Beginning 3-dc Cluster, finish off.

SPRING DAYS

With its simple pattern stitch, this gorgeous golden wrap welcomes the warmer days of spring. Flowing fringe along the ends gives the afghan wistful appeal.

Each Strip is worked across length of Afghan.

FIRST STRIP

Ch 5; dc in fifth ch from hook to form a ring.
Row 1 (Right side)**:** Slip st in ring, ch 3 **(counts as first dc, now and throughout)**, 4 dc in ring: 5 dc.
Note: Loop a short piece of yarn around any stitch to mark Row 1 as **right** side.
Row 2: Ch 4, turn; skip first 4 dc, sc in last dc.
Row 3: Ch 3, turn; 4 dc in ch-4 sp: 5 dc.
Repeat Rows 2 and 3 until Strip measures approximately 64½" from beginning ring, ending by working Row 3.
Last Row: Ch 5, turn; skip first 4 dc, slip st in last dc; do **not** finish off.
Strip Dividing Row: Do **not** turn; working in end of rows, slip st in first dc row, ch 3, 2 dc in same row, ★ ch 1, skip next row, 3 dc in next row; repeat from ★ across; do **not** finish off.

SECOND STRIP

Ch 5, turn; dc in fifth ch from hook to form a ring.
Row 1: Slip st in ring, ch 3, 4 dc in ring, skip first 3-dc group on Strip Dividing Row, slip st in next ch-1 sp: 5 dc.
Row 2: Ch 4, turn; skip first 4 dc on Strip, sc in last dc.
Row 3: Ch 3, turn; 4 dc in ch-4 sp, skip next 3-dc group on Strip Dividing Row, slip st in next ch-1 sp: 5 dc.
Repeat Rows 2 and 3 across to last 3-dc group on Strip Dividing Row, ending by working Row 2.
Next Row: Ch 3, turn; 4 dc in ch-4 sp, skip next 2 dc on Strip Dividing Row, slip st in last dc.
Last Row: Ch 5, turn; skip first 4 dc on Strip, slip st in last dc; do **not** finish off.
Strip Dividing Row: Do **not** turn; working in end of rows, slip st in first dc row, ch 3, 2 dc in same row, ★ ch 1, skip next row, 3 dc in next row; repeat from ★ across; do **not** finish off.

Repeat Second Strip until Afghan measures approximately 47" wide; do **not** finish off.

Continued on page 36.

Finished Size: 48½" x 65"

MATERIALS
Worsted Weight Yarn:
  48 ounces, (1,360 grams, 2,715 yards)
Crochet hook, size K (6.50 mm) **or** size needed for gauge

GAUGE: Each Strip = 2¼" wide;
    4 dc rows = 4"

WELCOME, BABY!

Welcome a new arrival with this sweet afghan! It's overflowing with beautiful springtime pastels. Popcorn stitches create the look of blossoming flowers.

Finished Size: 38" x 43"

MATERIALS
Worsted Weight Yarn:
    White - 8 ounces, (230 grams, 550 yards)
    Blue - 5 ounces, (140 grams, 345 yards)
    Pink - 5 ounces, (140 grams, 345 yards)
    Green - 5 ounces, (140 grams, 345 yards)
    Yellow - 2 ounces, (60 grams, 140 yards)
Crochet hook, size H (5.00 mm) **or** size needed
    for gauge

GAUGE: Each Center = 4" wide

STITCH GUIDE

> **V-STITCH (abbreviated V-St)**
> (Dc, ch 1, dc) in st or sp indicated.
> **POPCORN**
> 5 Dc in next sp, drop loop from hook, insert hook in first dc of 5-dc group, hook dropped loop and draw through. Push all Popcorns to **right** side.

PANEL (Make 7)

CENTER

Make 2 of **each** color: Blue, Pink, Green, and one Panel of Yellow.

Ch 22 **loosely**.
Row 1: Dc in fourth ch from hook, (skip next 2 chs, work V-St in next ch) across to last 3 chs, skip next 2 chs, 2 dc in last ch: 5 ch-1 sps.
Row 2 (Right side): Ch 3 **(counts as first dc, now and throughout)**, turn; dc in same st, work V-St in next ch-1 sp, ch 5, skip next ch-1 sp, sc in next ch-1 sp, ch 5, skip next ch-1 sp, work V-St in next ch-1 sp, skip next 2 dc, 2 dc in last st.
Note: Loop a short piece of yarn around any stitch to mark Row 2 as **right** side and bottom edge.

Row 3: Ch 3, turn; dc in same st, work V-St in next ch-1 sp, ch 3, (sc in next ch-5 sp, ch 3) twice, work V-St in next ch-1 sp, skip next 2 dc, 2 dc in last dc: 5 sps.
Row 4: Ch 3, turn; dc in same st, work V-St in next ch-1 sp, skip next ch-3 sp, work Popcorn in next ch-3 sp, (ch 2, work Popcorn) twice in same sp, ch 1, work V-St in next ch-1 sp, skip next 2 dc, 2 dc in last dc.
Row 5: Ch 3, turn; dc in same st, work V-St in next ch-1 sp, ch 3, skip next Popcorn, (sc in next ch-2 sp, ch 3) twice, work V-St in next ch-1 sp, skip next 2 dc, 2 dc in last dc: 5 sps.
Row 6: Ch 3, turn; dc in same st, work V-St in next ch-1 sp, work V-St in center ch of each of next 3 ch-3 sps, work V-St in next ch-1 sp, skip next 2 dc, 2 dc in last dc: 5 ch-1 sps.
Rows 7-86: Repeat Rows 2-6, 16 times.
Finish off.

BORDERS

Note: Work Right Side Border ONLY on first Blue Center. Work Left Side Border ONLY on second Blue Center. Work both Borders on remaining Centers.

RIGHT SIDE
Row 1: With **wrong** side facing, join White with slip st in end of Row 86; ch 1, work 172 sc evenly spaced across end of rows.
Row 2: Ch 1, turn; sc in each sc across; finish off.

LEFT SIDE
Row 1: With **wrong** side facing, join White with slip st in end of Row 1; ch 1, work 172 sc evenly spaced across end of rows.
Row 2: Ch 1, turn; sc in each sc across; finish off.

Continued on page 37.

BUDDING BEAUTY

*"Budding" with the splendor of spring, our blooming beauty
will add a fresh look to your decor. Treble and double crochet
clusters bring hearty texture to the eye-catching throw.*

Finished Size: 50" x 67"

MATERIALS
Worsted Weight Yarn:
    Green - 27½ ounces, (780 grams, 1,885 yards)
    Ecru - 23½ ounces, (670 grams, 1,610 yards)
Crochet hook, size I (5.50 mm) **or** size needed
    for gauge

GAUGE: In pattern, one repeat and 8 rows = 4"

Gauge Swatch: 8¼"w x 4"h
With Ecru, ch 26 **loosely**.
Work same as Afghan Body for 8 rows.

STITCH GUIDE

TREBLE CROCHET CLUSTER
    (abbreviated tr Cluster)
★ YO twice, insert hook in st indicated, YO and pull up a
loop, (YO and draw through 2 loops on hook) twice; repeat
from ★ once **more**, YO and draw through all 3 loops on
hook **(Figs. 15a & b, page 141)**.
FRONT POST DOUBLE CROCHET CLUSTER
    (abbreviated FPdc Cluster)
YO, insert hook from **front** to **back** around post of next tr
(Fig. 10, page 140), YO and pull up a loop, YO and draw
through 2 loops on hook, ★ YO, insert hook from **front** to
back around **same** st, YO and pull up a loop, YO and draw
through 2 loops on hook; repeat from ★ 2 times **more**, YO
and draw through all 5 loops on hook.

AFGHAN BODY

With Ecru, ch 146 **loosely**.
Row 1 (Right side)**:** Sc in second ch from hook, ★ ch 1, skip
next ch, sc in next ch; repeat from ★ across; finish off: 73 sc and
72 ch-1 sps.
Note: Loop a short piece of yarn around any stitch to mark
Row 1 as **right** side.

Row 2: With **wrong** side facing, join Green with slip st in first
sc; ch 6 **(counts as first tr plus ch 2, now and
throughout)**, work tr Cluster in same st, ch 1, skip next
ch-1 sp, (sc in next ch-1 sp, ch 1) 4 times, ★ skip next sc, work
(tr Cluster, ch 2, tr, ch 2, tr Cluster) in next sc, ch 1, skip next
ch-1 sp, (sc in next ch-1 sp, ch 1) 4 times; repeat from ★ across
to last 2 sc, skip next sc, work (tr Cluster, ch 2, tr) in last sc;
finish off: 85 sts and 84 sps.
Row 3: With **right** side facing, join Ecru with sc in first tr **(see
Joining With Sc, page 142)**; ch 1, (sc in next sp, ch 1) 7
times, ★ work FPdc Cluster, ch 1, (sc in next sp, ch 1) 7 times;
repeat from ★ across to last tr, sc in last tr; finish off:
11 FPdc Clusters, 86 sc, and 96 ch-1 sps.
Row 4: With **wrong** side facing, join Green with sc in first sc;
(sc in next ch-1 sp, ch 1) twice, skip next 2 sc, work (tr Cluster,
ch 2, tr, ch 2, tr Cluster) in next sc, ch 1, ★ skip next 2 ch-1 sps,
(sc in next ch-1 sp, ch 1) 4 times, skip next 2 sc, work
(tr Cluster, ch 2, tr, ch 2, tr Cluster) in next sc, ch 1; repeat from
★ across to last 4 ch-1 sps, skip next 2 ch-1 sps, sc in next
ch-1 sp, ch 1, sc in next ch-1 sp and in last sc; finish off: 86 sts
and 83 sps.
Row 5: With **right** side facing, join Ecru with sc in first sc; ch 1,
(sc in next sp, ch 1) 3 times, work FPdc Cluster, ch 1, ★ (sc in
next sp, ch 1) 7 times, work FPdc Cluster, ch 1; repeat from ★
across to last 3 sps, (sc in next sp, ch 1) 3 times, skip next sc, sc
in last sc; finish off: 12 FPdc Clusters, 85 sc, and 96 ch-1 sps.
Row 6: With **wrong** side facing, join Green with slip st in first
sc; ch 6, work tr Cluster in same st, ch 1, skip next 2 ch-1 sps,
(sc in next ch-1 sp, ch 1) 4 times, ★ skip next 2 sc, work
(tr Cluster, ch 2, tr, ch 2, tr Cluster) in next sc, ch 1, skip next
2 ch-1 sps, (sc in next ch-1 sp, ch 1) 4 times; repeat from ★
across to last 3 sc, skip next 2 sc, work (tr Cluster, ch 2, tr) in
last sc; finish off: 85 sts and 84 sps.
Row 7: With **right** side facing, join Ecru with sc in first tr; ch 1,
(sc in next sp, ch 1) 7 times, ★ work FPdc Cluster, ch 1, (sc in
next sp, ch 1) 7 times; repeat from ★ across to last tr, sc in last
tr; finish off: 11 FPdc Clusters, 86 sc, and 96 ch-1 sps.
Rows 8-133: Repeat Rows 4-7, 31 times; then repeat Rows 4
and 5 once **more**.

Continued on page 37.

33

POSY PATCH WRAP

Perky posies bloom all over this pretty afghan. The squares feature raised flower petals, and they come together quickly with a join-as-you-go method.

Finished Size: 47" x 67"

MATERIALS

Worsted Weight Yarn:

Ecru - 27 ounces, (770 grams, 1,530 yards)
Dk Green - 15 ounces, (430 grams, 850 yards)
Green - 9 ounces, (260 grams, 510 yards)
Blue - 6 ounces, (170 grams, 340 yards)
Yellow - 6 ounces, (170 grams, 340 yards)
Crochet hook, size F (3.75 mm) **or** size needed for gauge

GAUGE SWATCH: First Square = 4"
Work same as First Square.

FIRST STRIP

FIRST SQUARE

With Blue, ch 5; join with slip st to form a ring.

Rnd 1 (Right side)**:** Ch 1, (sc in ring, ch 5) 5 times; join with slip st to first sc, finish off: 5 petals.

Note: Loop a short piece of yarn around any stitch to mark Rnd 1 as **right** side.

Rnd 2: With **right** side facing and working **behind** petals, join Yellow with sc in beginning ring **between** any 2 sc *(see Joining With Sc, page 142)*; 2 sc in same sp, skip next sc, 2 sc in ring **before** next sc, skip next sc, 3 sc in ring **before** next sc, skip next sc, (2 sc in ring **before** next sc, skip next sc) twice; join with slip st to first sc, finish off: 12 sc.

Rnd 3: With **right** side facing and working **behind** petals, join Dk Green with sc in any sc on Rnd 2; ch 3, skip next 2 sc, ★ sc in next sc, ch 3, skip next 2 sc; repeat from ★ 2 times **more**; join with slip st to first sc, do **not** finish off: 4 ch-3 sps.

Rnd 4: Slip st in first ch-3 sp, ch 1, (sc, ch 3) twice in same sp and in each ch-3 sp around; join with slip st to first sc: 8 ch-3 sps.

Rnd 5: Slip st in first ch-3 sp, ch 1, sc in same sp, (2 dc, ch 3, 2 dc) in next ch-3 sp, ★ sc in next ch-3 sp, (2 dc, ch 3, 2 dc) in next ch-3 sp; repeat from ★ 2 times **more**; join with slip st to first sc, finish off: 20 sts and 4 ch-3 sps.

Rnd 6: With **right** side facing, join Green with sc in any corner ch-3 sp; ch 5, sc in same sp, ★ † ch 3, (skip next st, sc in next dc, ch 3) twice, skip next st †, (sc, ch 5, sc) in next corner ch-3 sp; repeat from ★ 2 times **more**, then repeat from † to † once; join with slip st to first sc, finish off: 12 ch-3 sps and 4 ch-5 sps.

Rnd 7: With **right** side facing, join Ecru with sc in any corner ch-5 sp; sc in same sp, ch 3, (2 sc in next ch-3 sp, ch 3) 3 times, ★ (2 sc, ch 3) twice in next corner ch-5 sp, (2 sc in next ch-3 sp, ch 3) 3 times; repeat from ★ 2 times **more**, 2 sc in same sp as first sc, ch 3; join with slip st to first sc, finish off: 20 ch-3 sps.

NEXT 15 SQUARES

Work same as First Square through Rnd 6: 12 ch-3 sps and 4 ch-5 sps.

Rnd 7 (Joining rnd)**:** With **right** side facing, join Ecru with sc in any corner ch-5 sp; sc in same sp, ch 3, (2 sc in next ch-3 sp, ch 3) 3 times, ★ (2 sc, ch 3) twice in next corner ch-5 sp, (2 sc in next ch-3 sp, ch 3) 3 times; repeat from ★ once **more**, 2 sc in next corner ch-5 sp, ch 1, holding Squares with **wrong** sides together, sc in corresponding corner ch-3 sp on **previous** Square *(Fig. 24, page 143)*, ch 1, 2 sc in same sp on **new** Square, ch 1, sc in next ch-3 sp on **previous** Square, ch 1, † 2 sc in next ch-3 sp on **new** Square, ch 1, sc in next ch-3 sp on **previous** Square, ch 1 †, repeat from † to † 2 times **more**, 2 sc in same sp as first sc on **new** Square, ch 1, sc in next corner ch-3 sp on **previous** Square, ch 1; join with slip st to first sc on **new** Square, finish off: 20 sps.

Continued on page 36.

EDGING

With **right** side of one short edge on Strip facing, join Ecru with sc in top right corner ch-3 sp; sc in same sp, ch 3, † (2 sc in next ch-3 sp, ch 3) 4 times, (2 sc, ch 3) twice in next corner ch-3 sp, (2 sc in next sp, ch 3) across to next corner ch-3 sp †, (2 sc, ch 3) twice in corner ch-3 sp, repeat from † to † once, 2 sc in same sp as first sc, ch 3; join with slip st to first sc, finish off: 204 ch-3 sps.

REMAINING 9 STRIPS

Work and join Squares in same manner as First Strip.

EDGING

Joining Rnd: With **right** side of one short edge on Strip facing, join Ecru with sc in top right corner ch-3 sp; sc in same sp, ch 3, (2 sc in next ch-3 sp, ch 3) 4 times, (2 sc, ch 3) twice in next corner ch-3 sp, (2 sc in next sp, ch 3) across to next corner ch-3 sp, (2 sc, ch 3) twice in corner ch-3 sp, (2 sc in next sp, ch 3) 4 times, 2 sc in next corner ch-3 sp, ch 1, holding Strips with **wrong** sides together, sc in corresponding corner ch-3 sp on **previous Strip**, ch 1, 2 sc in same sp on **new Strip**, ch 1, sc in next ch-3 sp on **previous Strip**, ch 1, ★ 2 sc in next sp on **new Strip**, ch 1, sc in next ch-3 sp on **previous Strip**, ch 1; repeat from ★ across, 2 sc in same sp as first sc on **new Strip**, ch 1, sc in next corner ch-3 sp on **previous Strip**, ch 1; join with slip st to first sc on **new Strip**, finish off: 204 sps.

SPRING DAYS Continued from page 28.

LAST STRIP

Ch 5, turn; dc in fifth ch from hook to form a ring.
Row 1: Slip st in ring, ch 3, 3 dc in ring, skip first 3-dc group on Strip Dividing Row, slip st in next ch-1 sp: 4 dc.
Row 2: Ch 4, turn; skip first 3 dc on Strip, sc in last dc.
Row 3: Ch 3, turn; 3 dc in ch-4 sp, skip next 3-dc group on Strip Dividing Row, slip st in next ch-1 sp: 4 dc.
Repeat Rows 2 and 3 across to last 3-dc group on Strip Dividing Row, ending by working Row 2.

Next Row: Ch 3, turn; 3 dc in ch-4 sp, skip next 2 dc on Strip Dividing Row, slip st in last dc.
Last Row: Ch 5, turn; skip first 3 dc on Strip, slip st in last dc; finish off.

Holding 8 strands of yarn together, each 16" long, add fringe in each sp across short edges of Afghan *(Figs. 27a & c, page 143)*.

WELCOME, BABY! Continued from page 30.

ASSEMBLY

Afghan is assembled by joining Panels in the following color sequence, from left to right: Blue with Right Side Border, Pink, Green, Yellow, Green, Pink, Blue with Left Side Border.
Join Panels as follows: Holding 2 Panels side by side with **right** sides facing and bottom edges at same end, join White with slip st in first sc at bottom edge of left Panel; ch 2, slip st in first sc on right Panel, ch 2, slip st in next sc on left Panel, ★ ch 2, skip next sc on right Panel, slip st in next sc, ch 2, skip next sc on left Panel, slip st in next sc; repeat from ★ across to last sc on right Panel, ch 2, sc in last sc; finish off.

Repeat for remaining Panels.

EDGING

Rnd 1: With **right** side facing, join White with slip st in top left corner; ch 1, 3 sc in same st; work 171 sc evenly spaced across end of rows to next corner; 3 sc in corner, work 129 sc evenly spaced across to next corner, 3 sc in corner; work 171 sc evenly spaced across end of rows to next corner; 3 sc in corner, work 129 sc evenly spaced across; join with slip st to first sc: 612 sc.
Rnd 2: Ch 1, turn; sc in same st and in each sc around, working (sc, ch 1, sc) in each corner sc; join with slip st to first sc.
Rnd 3: Turn; slip st in next sc, ch 1, sc in same st, ch 2, (sc, ch 2) twice in next corner ch-1 sp, sc in next sc, ★ (ch 2, skip next sc, sc in next sc) across to next corner ch-1 sp, ch 2, (sc, ch 2) twice in corner ch-1 sp, sc in next sc; repeat from ★ 2 times **more**, ch 2, skip next sc, (sc in next sc, ch 2, skip next st) across; join with slip st to first sc, finish off.

BUDDING BEAUTY Continued from page 32.

EDGING

Rnd 1: With **right** side facing, join Green with sc in first sc on Row 133; sc in same st, sc in next sc and in next ch-1 sp, sc in next 2 sc and in next FPdc Cluster, (work 11 sc evenly spaced across to next FPdc Cluster, sc in FPdc Cluster) 11 times, sc in next 2 sc, sc in next ch-1 sp and in next sc, 3 sc in last sc; sc evenly across end of rows; working in free loops of beginning ch **(Fig. 21b, page 142)**, 3 sc in first ch, sc in next 143 chs, 3 sc in next ch; sc evenly across end of rows and in same st as first sc; join with slip st to first sc.

Rnds 2 and 3: Ch 1, 2 sc in same st, ★ sc in next sc and in each sc across to center sc of next corner 3-sc group, 3 sc in center sc; repeat from ★ 2 times **more**, sc in next sc and in each sc across, sc in same st as first sc; join with slip st to first sc.
Finish off.

TEARDROP GARDEN

All the colors you'll find abloom in a springtime garden are assembled in this eye-catching afghan, which gets its attractive teardrop pattern from long double crochets. A tasseled fringe makes a delicate finish.

Finished Size: 49½" x 64"

MATERIALS
Worsted Weight Yarn:
  Ecru - 26½ ounces,
    (750 grams, 1,815 yards)
  Blue - 6 ounces,
    (170 grams, 410 yards)
  Rose - 6 ounces,
    (170 grams, 410 yards)
  Lavender - 6 ounces,
    (170 grams, 410 yards)
  Green - 6 ounces,
    (170 grams, 410 yards)
Crochet hook, size H (5.00 mm) **or** size
  needed for gauge

GAUGE: In pattern, 12 sts and
    8 rows = 3½"

Gauge Swatch: 4¼"w x 3½"h
Ch 18 **loosely**.
Work same as Afghan for 8 rows.

STITCH GUIDE

LONG DOUBLE CROCHET *(abbreviated LDC)*
YO, working **around** previous row, insert hook in ch-1 sp one row **below** next ch, YO and pull up a loop even with last dc made, (YO and draw through 2 loops on hook) twice *(Fig. 9, page 140)*.

AFGHAN

With Ecru, ch 174 **loosely**.

Row 1: Dc in sixth ch from hook and in next 4 chs, ★ ch 1, skip next ch, dc in next 5 chs; repeat from ★ across to last 2 chs, ch 1, skip next ch, dc in last ch: 141 dc and 29 sps.

Row 2 (Right side)**:** Ch 4 **(counts as first dc plus ch 1, now and throughout)**, turn; ★ skip next ch-1 sp, dc in next 5 dc, ch 1; repeat from ★ across to last sp, skip next ch, dc in next ch; finish off: 142 dc and 29 ch-1 sps.

Note: Loop a short piece of yarn around any stitch to mark Row 2 as **right** side.

Row 3: With **wrong** side facing, join Blue with slip st in first dc; ch 3 **(counts as first dc, now and throughout)**, work LDC, ★ dc in next 2 dc, ch 1, skip next dc, dc in next 2 dc, work LDC; repeat from ★ across to last dc, dc in last dc; do **not** finish off: 143 sts and 28 ch-1 sps.

Row 4: Ch 3, turn; dc in next 3 sts, ★ ch 1, skip next ch-1 sp, dc in next 5 sts; repeat from ★ across to last ch-1 sp, ch 1, skip last ch-1 sp, dc in last 4 sts; finish off.

Row 5: With **wrong** side facing, join Ecru with slip st in first dc; ch 4, ★ skip next dc, dc in next 2 dc, work LDC, dc in next 2 dc, ch 1; repeat from ★ across to last 2 dc, skip next dc, dc in last dc; do **not** finish off: 142 sts and 29 ch-1 sps.

Row 6: Ch 4, turn; ★ skip next ch-1 sp, dc in next 5 sts, ch 1; repeat from ★ across to last ch-1 sp, skip last ch-1 sp, dc in last dc; finish off.

Continued on page 47.

LOVELY IN LAVENDER

Lovely in lavender, this mile-a-minute throw was inspired by the beauty of springtime violas. Tuck it in a cozy corner retreat for a welcome respite from the day.

Finished Size: 45" x 64"

MATERIALS
Worsted Weight Yarn:
    32 ounces, (910 grams, 2,195 yards)
Crochet hook, size J (6.00 mm) **or** size needed
    for gauge

GAUGE: Each Strip = 4¹/₂ " wide

Gauge Swatch: 3" wide
Ch 11 **loosely**.
Row 1: Sc in second ch from hook and in each ch across:
10 sc.
Rows 2-5: Ch 1, turn; sc in each sc across.
Finish off.

STITCH GUIDE

SC DECREASE
Pull up a loop in next 2 sc, YO and draw through all 3 loops on hook **(counts as one sc)**.
DC DECREASE (uses next 2 sc)
★ YO, insert hook in **next** sc, YO and pull up a loop, YO and draw through 2 loops on hook; repeat from ★ once **more**, YO and draw through all 3 loops on hook **(counts as one dc)**.
PICOT
Ch 4, slip st in fourth ch from hook.

FIRST STRIP
Ch 192 **loosely**.
Foundation Row (Right side): Sc in back ridge of second ch from hook and each ch across *(Fig. 2b, page 139)*: 191 sc.
Note: Loop a short piece of yarn around any stitch to mark Foundation Row as **right** side.
Rnd 1: Slip st in end of Foundation Row, ch 4, [dc, ch 1, tr, (ch 1, dc) twice] in same row, ch 1; working in free loops of beginning ch *(Fig. 21b, page 142)*, † skip first 2 sts, sc in next st, ch 1, skip next 2 sts, ★ (dc, ch 1, tr, ch 1, dc) in next st, ch 1, skip next 2 sts, sc in next st, ch 1, skip next 2 sts; repeat from ★ 30 times **more** †; [(dc, ch 1) twice, tr, (ch 1, dc) twice] in end of Foundation Row, ch 1; working across sc on Foundation Row, repeat from † to † once; join with slip st to third ch of beginning ch-4: 260 ch-1 sps.
Rnd 2: Ch 1, sc in same st, † 2 sc in next ch-1 sp, sc in next dc, 2 sc in next ch-1 sp, 3 sc in next tr, (2 sc in next ch-1 sp, sc in next dc) twice, sc in next 2 ch-1 sps, ★ sc in next dc and in next ch-1 sp, 3 sc in next tr, sc in next ch-1 sp, sc in next dc and in next 2 ch-1 sps; repeat from ★ 30 times **more** †, sc in next dc, repeat from † to † once; join with slip st to first sc: 592 sc.
Rnd 3: Slip st in next sc, ch 2, dc in next sc, † (ch 2, dc decrease) twice, (dc, ch 3, dc) in next sc, (dc decrease, ch 2) 3 times, ★ skip next 4 sc, sc decrease, ch 2, (sc, ch 2) twice in next sc, sc decrease, ch 2; repeat from ★ 30 times **more**, skip next 4 sts †, dc decrease, repeat from † to † once; join with slip st to first dc: 260 sps.
Rnd 4: Ch 1, sc in same st, † [slip st in next ch-2 sp, (sc, ch 3, sc) in next dc] twice, slip st in next dc, ch 3, (dc, work Picot, dc) in next ch-3 sp, ch 3, slip st in next dc, (sc, ch 3, sc) in next dc, [slip st in next ch-2 sp, (sc, ch 3, sc) in next dc] twice, ch 3, skip next ch-2 sp, ★ sc in next ch-2 sp, (sc, ch 1, sc) in next ch-2 sp, sc in next ch-2 sp, ch 3, skip next ch-2 sp; repeat from ★ 30 times **more** †, (sc, ch 3, sc) in next dc, repeat from † to † once, sc in same st as first sc, ch 3; join with slip st to first sc, finish off: 142 sps.

Continued on page 47.

GRANDMOTHER'S GARDEN

All of the charm of Grandmother's flower garden is gathered in this richly colored spread, designed for year-round beauty. Worsted weight yarn yields the bountiful blooms, which are assembled following our easy placement chart.

Finished Size: 51" x 67"

MATERIALS

Worsted Weight Yarn:
- Rose - 21 ounces, (600 grams, 1,440 yards)
- Green - 18 ounces, (510 grams, 1,235 yards)
- Lt Rose - 11 ounces, (310 grams, 755 yards)
- Yellow - 2 ounces, (60 grams, 135 yards)

Crochet hook, size G (4.00 mm) **or** size needed for gauge

GAUGE SWATCH: 1³/₄ " (straight edge to straight edge)
Work same as First Motif.

FLOWER (Make 28)
MOTIFS
FIRST

With Yellow, ch 6; join with slip st to form a ring.

Rnd 1 (Right side)**:** Ch 6 **(counts as first dc plus ch 3)**, (dc in ring, ch 3) 5 times; join with slip st to first dc: 6 ch-3 sps.

Note: Loop a short piece of yarn around any stitch to mark Rnd 1 as **right** side.

Rnd 2: Slip st in first ch-3 sp, ch 1, (2 sc, ch 3, 2 sc) in same sp and in each ch-3 sp around; join with slip st to first sc, finish off.

Using Placement Chart as a guide, work Second through 19th Motifs.

PLACEMENT CHART

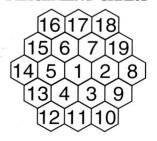

SECOND

With Lt Rose, work same as First Motif through Rnd 1: 6 ch-3 sps.

Rnd 2 (Joining rnd)**:** Slip st in first ch-3 sp, ch 1, (2 sc, ch 3, 2 sc) in same sp and in next 3 ch-3 sps, 2 sc in next ch-3 sp, ch 1, holding Motifs with **wrong** sides together, sc in any ch-3 sp on **adjacent Motif** *(Fig. 24, page 143)*, ch 1, 2 sc in same sp on **new Motif** and in next ch-3 sp, ch 1, sc in next ch-3 sp on **adjacent Motif**, ch 1, 2 sc in same sp on **new Motif**; join with slip st to first sc, finish off.

THIRD THROUGH SIXTH

With Lt Rose, work same as First Motif through Rnd 1: 6 ch-3 sps.

Rnd 2 (Joining rnd)**:** Slip st in first ch-3 sp, ch 1, (2 sc, ch 3, 2 sc) in same sp and in next 2 ch-3 sps, 2 sc in next ch-3 sp, ch 1, holding Motifs with **wrong** sides together, sc in first ch-3 sp to right of previous joining on **adjacent Motif**, ch 1, 2 sc in same sp on **new Motif** and in next ch-3 sp, ch 1, sc in next joining sc on **adjacent Motif**, ch 1, 2 sc in same sp on **new Motif** and in next ch-3 sp, ch 1, sc in next ch-3 sp on **adjacent Motif**, ch 1, 2 sc in same sp on **new Motif**; join with slip st to first sc, finish off.

SEVENTH

With Lt Rose, work same as First Motif through Rnd 1: 6 ch-3 sps.

Rnd 2 (Joining rnd)**:** Slip st in first ch-3 sp, ch 1, (2 sc, ch 3, 2 sc) in same sp and in next ch-3 sp, 2 sc in next ch-3 sp, ch 1, holding Motifs with **wrong** sides together, sc in first ch-3 sp to right of previous joining on **adjacent Motif**, ch 1, 2 sc in same sp on **new Motif** and in next ch-3 sp, ch 1, ★ sc in next joining sc on **adjacent Motif**, ch 1, 2 sc in same sp on **new Motif** and in next ch-3 sp, ch 1; repeat from ★ once **more**, sc in next ch-3 sp on **adjacent Motif**, ch 1, 2 sc in same sp on **new Motif**; join with slip st to first sc, finish off.

Continued on page 48.

DREAMY FLOWERS

This dreamy afghan will enrich your home with the timeless beauty of flowers. The delicate bud motifs are worked separately in simple stitches to create the textured pattern and then joined as you go.

Finished Size: 49" x 69"

MATERIALS

Worsted Weight Yarn:
  57 ounces, (1,620 grams, 3,910 yards)
Crochet hook, size H (5.00 mm) **or** size needed
  for gauge

GAUGE: Each Motif = 4¹/₂ " diameter

Gauge Swatch: 3³/₄ " diameter
Work same as First Motif through Rnd 3.

STITCH GUIDE

DECREASE
Insert hook from **front** to **back** through next ch-1 sp, skip next 4 ch-1 sps, insert hook from **back** to **front** through next ch-1 sp, YO and pull up a loop, YO and draw through both loops on hook.

FIRST MOTIF

Rnd 1: Ch 6, slip st in sixth ch from hook, (ch 5, slip st in same ch) 5 times: 6 ch-5 sps.
Rnd 2 (Right side): [Sc, ch 1, (dc, ch 1) 7 times, sc] in each ch-5 sp around; join with slip st to first sc: 42 dc and 48 ch-1 sps.
Note: Loop a short piece of yarn around any stitch to mark Rnd 2 as **right** side.
Rnd 3: Slip st in first ch-1 sp, (slip st in next dc and in next ch-1 sp) 3 times, ch 1, sc in same sp, ch 3, sc in next ch-1 sp, ch 3, decrease, ★ ch 3, (sc in next ch-1 sp, ch 3) twice, decrease; repeat from ★ 4 times **more**, ch 1, hdc in first sc to form last ch-3 sp: 18 ch-3 sps.
Rnd 4: Ch 1, sc in same sp, (ch 3, sc in next ch-3 sp) twice, ch 5, ★ sc in next ch-3 sp, (ch 3, sc in next ch-3 sp) twice, ch 5; repeat from ★ around; join with slip st to first sc, finish off: 6 ch-5 sps and 12 ch-3 sps.

ADDITIONAL MOTIFS

Rnds 1-3: Work same as First Motif: 18 ch-3 sps.
Rnd 4 (Joining rnd): Following Placement Diagram, page 46, work One, Two, or Three Side Joining.

ONE SIDE JOINING

Rnd 4 (Joining rnd): Ch 1, sc in same sp, (ch 3, sc in next ch-3 sp) twice, ★ ch 5, sc in next ch-3 sp, (ch 3, sc in next ch-3 sp) twice; repeat from ★ 3 times **more**, ch 2, holding Motifs with **wrong** sides together, slip st in third ch of corresponding ch-5 on **adjacent Motif** *(Fig. 24, page 143)*, ch 2, sc in next ch-3 sp on **new Motif**, (ch 1, sc in next ch-3 sp on **adjacent Motif**, ch 1, sc in next ch-3 sp on **new Motif**) twice, ch 2, slip st in third ch of next ch-5 on **adjacent Motif**, ch 2; join with slip st to first sc on **new Motif**, finish off.

TWO SIDE JOINING

Rnd 4 (Joining rnd): Ch 1, sc in same sp, (ch 3, sc in next ch-3 sp) twice, ★ ch 5, sc in next ch-3 sp, (ch 3, sc in next ch-3 sp) twice; repeat from ★ 2 times **more**, ch 2, holding Motifs with **wrong** sides together and working in first ch-5 to right of previous joining on **adjacent Motif**, slip st in third ch of ch-5 on **adjacent Motif**, † ch 2, sc in next ch-3 sp on **new Motif**, (ch 1, sc in next ch-3 sp on **adjacent Motif**, ch 1, sc in next ch-3 sp on **new Motif**) twice, ch 2 †, slip st in same ch as previous joining on **adjacent Motif**, repeat from † to † once, slip st in third ch of next ch-5 on **adjacent Motif**, ch 2; join with slip st to first sc on **new Motif**, finish off.

THREE SIDE JOINING

Rnd 4 (Joining rnd): Ch 1, sc in same sp, (ch 3, sc in next ch-3 sp) twice, [ch 5, sc in next ch-3 sp, (ch 3, sc in next ch-3 sp) twice] 2 times, ch 2, holding Motifs with **wrong** sides together and working in first ch-5 to right of previous joining on **adjacent Motif**, slip st in third ch of ch-5 on **adjacent Motif**, ch 2, ★ † sc in next ch-3 sp on **new Motif**, (ch 1, sc in next ch-3 sp on **adjacent Motif**, ch 1, sc in next ch-3 sp on **new Motif**) twice, ch 2 †, slip st in same ch as previous joining on **adjacent Motif**, ch 2; repeat from ★ once **more**, then repeat from † to † once, slip st in third ch of next ch-5 on **adjacent Motif**, ch 2; join with slip st to first sc on **new Motif**, finish off.

Continued on page 46.

PLACEMENT DIAGRAM

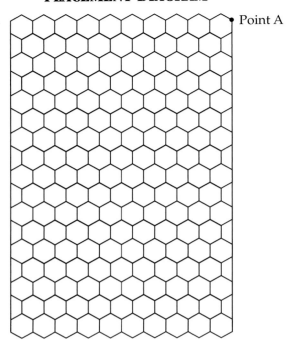

• Point A

HALF MOTIF

Row 1: Ch 5, dc in fifth ch from hook, (ch 1, dc in same ch) 4 times: 5 sps.

Row 2 (Right side): Ch 4, turn; dc in first ch-1 sp, ch 1, dc in next dc, ★ ch 1, dc in next ch-1 sp, ch 1, dc in next dc; repeat from ★ 2 times **more**, ch 4, skip next ch, slip st in next ch: 9 sps.

Note: Mark Row 2 as **right** side.

Row 3 (Joining row): Ch 1, do **not** turn; sc in end of first row, (ch 3, sc in end of next row) twice, ch 2; following Placement Diagram, holding Motifs with **wrong** sides together and working in first ch-5 to right of previous joining on **adjacent Motif**, slip st in third ch of ch-5 on **adjacent Motif**, ch 2, sc in same sp on **Half Motif**, (ch 1, sc in next ch-3 sp on **adjacent Motif**, ch 1, sc in next ch-1 sp on **Half Motif**) twice, ch 2, ★ slip st in same ch as previous joining on **adjacent Motif**, ch 2, sc in next ch-1 sp on **Half Motif**, (ch 1, sc in next ch-3 sp on **adjacent Motif**, ch 1, sc in next sp on **Half Motif**) twice, ch 2; repeat from ★ once **more**, slip st in third ch of next ch-5 on **adjacent Motif**, ch 2, sc in same sp on **Half Motif**, ch 3; join with slip st to first sc, finish off.

Repeat for remaining 15 Half Motifs.

EDGING

Rnd 1: With **right** side facing, join yarn with sc in ch-5 sp at Point A *(see Joining With Sc, page 142)*; ch 3, sc in same sp, ch 3, † (sc in next ch-3 sp, ch 3) twice, (sc, ch 3) twice in next ch-5 sp, (sc in next ch-3 sp, ch 3) twice, ★ skip next ch-2 sp, sc in next joining, ch 3, skip next ch-2 sp, (sc in next ch-3 sp, ch 3) twice, (sc, ch 3) twice in next ch-5 sp, (sc in next ch-3 sp, ch 3) twice; repeat from ★ 8 times **more**, (sc, ch 3) twice in next ch-5 sp, (sc in next sp, ch 3) across to next ch-5 sp †, (sc, ch 3) twice in ch-5 sp, repeat from † to † once; join with slip st to first sc: 294 ch-3 sps.

Rnd 2: (Slip st, ch 2, hdc) in each ch-3 sp around; join with slip st to first slip st.

Rnd 3: Slip st in first ch-2 sp, ch 1, (sc, ch 3) twice in same sp and in next 6 ch-2 sps, † (sc in next ch-2 sp, ch 3) twice, ★ (sc, ch 3) twice in next 5 ch-2 sps, (sc in next ch-2 sp, ch 3) twice; repeat from ★ 7 times **more** †, (sc, ch 3) twice in next 89 ch-2 sps, repeat from † to † once, (sc, ch 3, sc) in next ch-2 sp, (ch 3, sc) twice in next ch-2 sp and in each ch-2 sp across, ch 1, hdc in first sc to form last ch-3 sp: 552 ch-3 sps.

Rnds 4 and 5: Ch 1, sc in same sp, (ch 3, sc in next ch-3 sp) around, ch 1, hdc in first sc to form last ch-3 sp.

Rnd 6: Ch 1, sc in same sp, ch 3, dc in third ch from hook, ★ sc in next ch-3 sp, ch 3, dc in third ch from hook; repeat from ★ around; join with slip st to first sc, finish off.

INNER EDGING

With **right** side facing, working in **front** of Border and in slip sts on Rnd 2, join yarn with sc in any slip st; ch 3, dc in third ch from hook, ★ sc in next slip st, ch 3, dc in third ch from hook; repeat from ★ around; join with slip st to first sc, finish off.

TEARDROP GARDEN Continued from page 38.

Row 7: With **wrong** side facing, join Rose with slip st in first dc; ch 3, work LDC, ★ dc in next 2 dc, ch 1, skip next dc, dc in next 2 dc, work LDC; repeat from ★ across to last dc, dc in last dc; do **not** finish off: 143 sts and 28 ch-1 sps.

Row 8: Ch 3, turn; dc in next 3 sts, ★ ch 1, skip next ch-1 sp, dc in next 5 sts; repeat from ★ across to last ch-1 sp, ch 1, skip last ch-1 sp, dc in last 4 sts; finish off.

Row 9: With **wrong** side facing, join Ecru with slip st in first dc; ch 4, ★ skip next dc, dc in next 2 dc, work LDC, dc in next 2 dc, ch 1; repeat from ★ across to last 2 dc, skip next dc, dc in last dc; do **not** finish off: 142 sts and 29 ch-1 sps.

Row 10: Ch 4, turn; ★ skip next ch-1 sp, dc in next 5 sts, ch 1; repeat from ★ across to last ch-1 sp, skip last ch-1 sp, dc in last dc; finish off.

Rows 11 and 12: With Lavender, repeat Rows 7 and 8.

Rows 13 and 14: Repeat Rows 9 and 10.

Rows 15 and 16: With Green, repeat Rows 7 and 8.

Rows 17 and 18: Repeat Rows 9 and 10.

Repeat Rows 3-18 until Afghan measures approximately 64" from beginning ch, ending by working 2 rows with Ecru.

Holding 7 strands of Ecru together, each 22" long, add fringe in sps across short edges of Afghan *(Figs. 27a & c, page 143)*.

LOVELY IN LAVENDER Continued from page 40.

REMAINING 9 STRIPS

Work same as First Strip through Rnd 3: 260 sps.

Rnd 4 (Joining rnd): Ch 1, sc in same st, ✝ [slip st in next ch-2 sp, (sc, ch 3, sc) in next dc] twice, slip st in next dc, ch 3, (dc, work Picot, dc) in next ch-3 sp, ch 3, slip st in next dc, (sc, ch 3, sc) in next dc ✝, [slip st in next ch-2 sp, (sc, ch 3, sc) in next dc] twice, ch 3, [skip next ch-2 sp, sc in next ch-2 sp, (sc, ch 1, sc) in next ch-2 sp, sc in next ch-2 sp, ch 3] 31 times, skip next ch-2 sp, (sc, ch 3, sc) in next dc, repeat from ✝ to ✝ once, slip st in next ch-2 sp, (sc, ch 3, sc) in next dc, slip st in next ch-2 sp, sc in next dc, ch 1, holding Strips with **wrong** sides together, slip st in corresponding ch-3 sp on **previous Strip** *(Fig. 24, page 143)*, ch 1, sc in same st on **new Strip**, ch 3, skip next ch-2 sp, ★ sc in next 2 ch-2 sps, skip next ch-3 sp on **previous Strip**, slip st in next ch-1 sp, sc in same sp on **new Strip** and in next ch-2 sp, ch 3, skip next ch-2 sp; repeat from ★ 30 times **more**, sc in same st as first sc, ch 1, skip next ch-3 sp on **previous Strip**, slip st in next ch-3 sp, ch 1; join with slip st to first sc, finish off.

EIGHTH

With Rose, work same as First Motif through Rnd 1: 6 ch-3 sps.

Rnd 2 (Joining rnd): Slip st in first ch-3 sp, ch 1, (2 sc, ch 3, 2 sc) in same sp and in next 2 ch-3 sps, place marker around last ch-3 made for Assembly Placement, (2 sc, ch 3, 2 sc) in next ch-3 sp, 2 sc in next ch-3 sp, ch 1, holding Motifs with **wrong** sides together, sc in first ch-3 sp to left of previous joining on **adjacent Motif**, ch 1, 2 sc in same sp on **new Motif** and in next ch-3 sp, ch 1, sc in next ch-3 sp on **adjacent Motif**, ch 1, 2 sc in same sp on **new Motif**; join with slip st to first sc, finish off.

NINTH

With Rose, work same as Seventh Motif.

TENTH

With Rose, work same as Third Motif.

11TH

With Rose, work same as Seventh Motif.

12TH

With Rose, work same as Third Motif.

13TH

With Rose, work same as Seventh Motif.

14TH

With Rose, work same as Third Motif.

15TH

With Rose, work same as Seventh Motif.

16TH

With Rose, work same as Third Motif.

17TH

With Rose, work same as Seventh Motif.

18TH

With Rose, work same as Third Motif.

19TH

With Rose, work same as First Motif through Rnd 1: 6 ch-3 sps.

Rnd 2 (Joining rnd): Slip st in first ch-3 sp, ch 1, (2 sc, ch 3, 2 sc) in same sp, 2 sc in next ch-3 sp, ch 1, holding Motifs with **wrong** sides together, sc in first ch-3 sp to right of previous joining on **last Motif** made, ch 1, 2 sc in same sp on **new Motif** and in next ch-3 sp, ch 1, ★ sc in next joining sc on **adjacent Motif**, ch 1, 2 sc in same sp on **new Motif** and in next ch-3 sp, ch 1; repeat from ★ 2 times **more**, sc in next ch-3 sp on **adjacent Motif**, ch 1, 2 sc in same sp on **new Motif**; join with slip st to first sc, finish off.

ASSEMBLY

MOTIFS

With Green, work same as First Motif through Rnd 1: 6 ch-3 sps.

Rnd 2 (Joining rnd): Using Placement Diagram as a guide and beginning at Point A, work Three, Four, Five, or Six Point Joining.

THREE POINT JOINING

Rnd 2 (Joining rnd): Slip st in first ch-3 sp, ch 1, (2 sc, ch 3, 2 sc) in same sp and in next 2 ch-3 sps, 2 sc in next ch-3 sp, ch 1, holding Motifs with **wrong** sides together, sc in first ch-3 sp to right of previous joining on **adjacent Motif**, ch 1, 2 sc in same sp on **new Motif** and in next ch-3 sp, ch 1, sc in next joining sc on **adjacent Motif**, ch 1, 2 sc in same sp on **new Motif** and in next ch-3 sp, ch 1, sc in next ch-3 sp on **adjacent Motif**, ch 1, 2 sc in same sp on **new Motif**; join with slip st to first sc, finish off.

FOUR POINT JOINING

Rnd 2 (Joining rnd): Slip st in first ch-3 sp, ch 1, (2 sc, ch 3, 2 sc) in same sp and in next ch-3 sp, 2 sc in next ch-3 sp, ch 1, holding Motifs with **wrong** sides together, sc in first ch-3 sp to right of previous joining on **adjacent Motif**, ch 1, 2 sc in same sp on **new Motif** and in next ch-3 sp, ch 1, ★ sc in next joining sc on **adjacent Motif**, ch 1, 2 sc in same sp on **new Motif** and in next ch-3 sp, ch 1; repeat from ★ once **more**, sc in next ch-3 sp on **adjacent Motif**, ch 1, 2 sc in same sp on **new Motif**; join with slip st to first sc, finish off.

FIVE POINT 2 FLOWER JOINING

Rnd 2 (Joining rnd)**:** Slip st in first ch-3 sp, ch 1, (2 sc, ch 3, 2 sc) in same sp, 2 sc in next ch-3 sp, ch 1, holding Motifs with **wrong** sides together, sc in first ch-3 sp to right of previous joining on **adjacent Motif**, ch 1, 2 sc in same sp on **new Motif** and in next ch-3 sp, ch 1, sc in next joining sc on **adjacent Motif**, ch 1, 2 sc in same sp on **new Motif** and in next ch-3 sp, ch 1, sc in next ch-3 sp on **adjacent Motif**, ch 1, 2 sc in same sp on **new Motif** and in next ch-3 sp, ch 1, holding **wrong** sides of previous Flower and next Flower together, sc in marked ch-3 sp on **next Flower**, ch 1, 2 sc in same sp on **new Motif** and in next ch-3 sp, ch 1, sc in next ch-3 sp on **adjacent Motif**, ch 1, 2 sc in same sp on **new Motif**; join with slip st to first sc, finish off.

SIX POINT 2 FLOWER JOINING

Rnd 2 (Joining rnd)**:** Slip st in first ch-3 sp, ch 1, 2 sc in same sp, ch 1, holding Motifs with **wrong** sides together, sc in first ch-3 sp to right of previous joining on **new Flower**, ch 1, 2 sc in same sp on **new Motif** and in next ch-3 sp, ch 1, ★ sc in next joining sc on **adjacent Motif**, ch 1, 2 sc in same sp on **new Motif** and in next ch-3 sp, ch 1; repeat from ★ 3 times **more**, sc in next ch-3 sp on **adjacent Motif**, ch 1, 2 sc in same sp on **new Motif**; join with slip st to first sc, finish off.

SIX POINT 3 FLOWER JOINING

Rnd 2 (Joining rnd)**:** Slip st in first ch-3 sp, ch 1, 2 sc in same sp, ch 1, holding Motifs with **wrong** sides together, sc in first ch-3 sp to right of previous joining on **previous Flower**, ch 1, 2 sc in same sp on **new Motif** and in next ch-3 sp, ch 1, ★ sc in next joining sc on **adjacent Motif**, ch 1, 2 sc in same sp on **new Motif** and in next ch-3 sp, ch 1; repeat from ★ once **more**, sc in next ch-3 sp on **adjacent Motif**, 2 sc in same sp on **new Motif** and in next ch-3 sp, ch 1, holding **wrong** sides of previous 2 Flowers and next Flower together, sc in marked ch-3 sp on **next Flower**, ch 1, 2 sc in same sp on **new Motif** and in next ch-3 sp, ch 1, sc in next ch-3 sp on **adjacent Motif**, ch 1, 2 sc in same sp on **new Motif**; join with slip st to first sc, finish off.

PLACEMENT DIAGRAM

Point A

MAY JEWELS

Black yarn provides a dramatic backdrop for the floral motifs in this wrap, which works up quickly holding two strands of yarn. Crocheted in rich jewel tones, the dazzling blooms are sure to win your heart.

Finished Size: 46" x 64"

MATERIALS
Worsted Weight Yarn:
Black - 48 ounces,
(1,360 grams, 2,710 yards)
Variegated - 16 ounces,
(450 grams, 930 yards)
Turquoise - 14 ounces,
(400 grams, 760 yards)
Crochet hook, size P (10.00 mm) **or** size
needed for gauge
Yarn needle

Entire Afghan is worked holding two strands of yarn together.

GAUGE: Each Motif = 5³/4 " (straight edge to straight edge)

Gauge Swatch: 3¹/2" diameter
Work same as Motif through Rnd 2.

MOTIF (Make 95)

With Variegated, ch 4; join with slip st to form a ring.
Rnd 1 (Wrong side): Ch 1, (sc, tr) 6 times in ring; join with slip st to first sc, finish off: 12 sts.
Note: Loop a short piece of yarn around **back** of any stitch to mark **right** side.
Rnd 2: With **wrong** side facing, join Turquoise with sc in any sc **(see Joining With Sc, page 142)**; (tr, sc) in same st, skip next tr, ★ (sc, tr, sc) in next sc, skip next tr; repeat from ★ around; join with slip st to first sc, finish off: 18 sts.
Rnd 3: With **right** side facing, join Black with sc in any tr; 2 sc in same st, hdc in next 2 sc, (3 sc in next tr, hdc in next 2 sc) around; join with slip st to first sc, do **not** finish off: 30 sts.
Rnd 4: Ch 1, turn; sc in same st and in next 3 sts, (sc, tr, sc) in next sc, ★ sc in next 4 sts, (sc, tr, sc) in next sc; repeat from ★ around; join with slip st to first sc, finish off: 42 sts.

ASSEMBLY

With Black, using Placement Diagram as a guide, and working through inside loops only, whipstitch Motifs together **(Fig. 26a, page 143)**, forming 5 vertical strips of 11 Motifs each and 4 vertical strips of 10 Motifs each, beginning in any tr and ending in next tr; whipstitch strips together in same manner.

PLACEMENT DIAGRAM

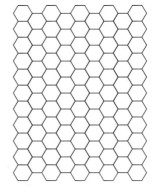

EDGING

With **wrong** side facing and working in Front Loops Only **(Fig. 20, page 142)**, join Black with sc in any st; sc in next st and in each st around; join with slip st to **both** loops of first sc, finish off.

FLOWERS FOR BABY

This flower-strewn blanket for baby will be a favorite for years to come! Worked in soothing shades of sport weight yarn, dainty floral curls nestle in creamy squares skirted with a lovely ruffle.

Finished Size: 37" x 46"

MATERIALS

Sport Weight Yarn:
  White - 23 ounces, (650 grams, 1,840 yards)
  Pink - 8 ounces, (230 grams, 640 yards)
  Green - 5½ ounces, (160 grams, 440 yards)
Crochet hook, size G (4.00 mm) **or** size needed for gauge
Yarn needle

GAUGE SWATCH: 4¼"
Work same as Square.

STITCH GUIDE

CURLIQUE
Ch 4, working under top loop and back ridge of chs *(Fig. 2c, page 139)*, 3 sc in second ch from hook and in each of last 2 chs.

LARGE CURLIQUE
Ch 5, working under top loop and back ridge of chs, 2 dc in third ch from hook, 3 dc in each of last 2 chs.

SQUARE (Make 80)

Rnd 1 (Right side): With Pink, ch 2, 8 sc in second ch from hook; join with slip st to first sc.

Note: Loop a short piece of yarn around any stitch to mark Rnd 1 as **right** side.

Rnd 2: Ch 1, sc in same st, work Curlique, (sc in next sc, work Curlique) around; join with slip st to first sc: 8 Curliques and 8 sc.

Rnd 3: Ch 1, sc in same st, ch 3, keeping Curliques to **front** of work, sc in next sc, ch 1, ★ sc in next sc, ch 3, sc in next sc, ch 1; repeat from ★ 2 times **more**; join with slip st to first sc, finish off.

Rnd 4: With **wrong** side facing, join Green with sc in any ch-3 sp *(see Joining With Sc, page 142)*; work Large Curlique, sc in same sp, ch 3, skip next ch-1 sp, ★ (sc, work Large Curlique, sc) in next ch-3 sp, ch 3, skip next ch-1 sp; repeat from ★ 2 times **more**; join with slip st to first sc, finish off: 4 Large Curliques and 4 ch-3 sps.

Rnd 5: With **right** side facing, join White with sc in first sc to **right** of any Large Curlique; ★ † working **behind** next Large Curlique, (dc, ch 3, dc) in ch-3 sp on Rnd 3 (between sc), sc in next sc on Rnd 4, working in **front** of next ch-3 and in sts and sps on Rnd 3, dc in next sc, dc in next ch-1 sp and in next sc †, sc in next sc on Rnd 4; repeat from ★ 2 times **more**, then repeat from † to † once; join with slip st to first sc: 28 sts and 4 ch-3 sps.

Rnd 6: Ch 3 **(counts as first dc)**, dc in next dc, (2 dc, ch 3, 2 dc) in next ch-3 sp, ★ dc in next 7 sts, (2 dc, ch 3, 2 dc) in next ch-3 sp; repeat from ★ 2 times **more**, dc in last 5 sts; join with slip st to first dc: 44 dc and 4 ch-3 sps.

Rnd 7: Slip st in next dc, ch 4 **(counts as first dc plus ch 1, now and throughout)**, skip next dc, dc in next dc, ch 1, (dc, ch 3, dc) in next ch-3 sp, ch 1, ★ dc in next dc, ch 1, (skip next dc, dc in next dc, ch 1) 5 times, (dc, ch 3, dc) in next ch-3 sp, ch 1; repeat from ★ 2 times **more**, (dc in next dc, ch 1, skip next dc) 4 times; join with slip st to first dc, finish off: 32 dc and 32 sps.

ASSEMBLY

With White, and working though both loops, whipstitch Squares together *(Fig. 26b, page 143)*, forming 8 vertical strips of 10 Squares each, beginning in center ch of first corner ch-3 and ending in center ch of next corner ch-3; whipstitch strips together in same manner.

EDGING

Rnd 1: With **wrong** side facing, join White with sc in any corner ch-3 sp; ch 3, sc in same sp, ch 1, (sc in next sp, ch 1) across to next corner ch-3 sp, ★ (sc, ch 3, sc) in corner ch-3 sp, ch 1, (sc in next sp, ch 1) across to next corner ch-3 sp; repeat from ★ 2 times **more**; join with slip st to first sc, do **not** finish off: 324 sc and 324 sps.

Continued on page 61.

53

SPIDER LACE

As splendid as a beautifully spun spider web, the delicate pattern
of this lovely wrap is nicely complemented by a captivating edging.
A soft shade of rose gives the lacy cover-up a romantic air.

Finished Size: 52" x 70"

MATERIALS
   Worsted Weight Yarn:
      42 ounces, (1,190 grams, 2,380 yards)
      Crochet hook, size I (5.50 mm) **or** size needed
         for gauge

GAUGE: One repeat and 6 rows = 2¼"

Gauge Swatch: 7"w x 4"h
Ch 23 **loosely**.
Work same as Afghan Body for 10 rows.
Finish off.

AFGHAN BODY

Ch 156 **loosely**.
Row 1 (Right side): Sc in second ch from hook and in each ch
across: 155 sc.
Row 2: Ch 1, turn; sc in first 3 sc, ch 5, (skip next 2 sc, sc in
next 5 sc, ch 5) across to last 5 sc, skip next 2 sc, sc in last
3 sc: 22 ch-5 sps.
Row 3: Ch 1, turn; sc in first 2 sc, ch 3, sc in next ch-5 sp,
ch 3, ★ skip next sc, sc in next 3 sc, ch 3, sc in next ch-5 sp,
ch 3; repeat from ★ across to last 3 sc, skip next sc, sc in last
2 sc: 44 ch-3 sps.
Row 4: Ch 1, turn; sc in first sc, ★ ch 3, sc in next ch-3 sp, sc
in next sc and in next ch-3 sp, ch 3, skip next sc, sc in next sc;
repeat from ★ across.
Row 5: Ch 5 **(counts as first dc plus ch 2)**, turn; sc in next
ch-3 sp, sc in next 3 sc and in next ch-3 sp, ★ ch 5, sc in next
ch-3 sp, sc in next 3 sc and in next ch-3 sp; repeat from ★
across to last sc, ch 2, dc in last sc: 21 ch-5 sps.
Row 6: Ch 1, turn; sc in first dc, ch 3, skip next sc, sc in next
3 sc, ch 3, ★ sc in next ch-5 sp, ch 3, skip next sc, sc in next
3 sc, ch 3; repeat from ★ across to last dc, sc in last dc:
44 ch-3 sps.

Row 7: Ch 1, turn; sc in first sc, ★ sc in next ch-3 sp, ch 3, skip
next sc, sc in next sc, ch 3, sc in next ch-3 sp and in next sc;
repeat from ★ across.
Row 8: Ch 1, turn; sc in first 2 sc and in next ch-3 sp, ch 5, sc
in next ch-3 sp, ★ sc in next 3 sc and in next ch-3 sp, ch 5, sc in
next ch-3 sp; repeat from ★ across to last 2 sc, sc in last 2 sc:
22 ch-5 sps.
Rows 9-169: Repeat Rows 3-8, 26 times; then repeat Rows 3-7
once **more**.
Row 170: Ch 1, turn; sc in first 2 sc and in next ch-3 sp, ch 2,
sc in next ch-3 sp, ★ sc in next 3 sc and in next ch-3 sp, ch 2, sc
in next ch-3 sp; repeat from ★ across to last 2 sc, sc in last 2 sc:
22 ch-2 sps.
Row 171: Ch 1, turn; sc in each sc and in each ch across; do
not finish off: 155 sc.

EDGING

Rnd 1: Ch 1, do **not** turn; work 173 sc evenly spaced across
end of rows, ch 2; working in free loops of beginning ch
(Fig. 21b, page 142), 2 sc in first ch, sc in next 153 chs, 2 sc
in next ch, ch 2; work 173 sc evenly spaced across end of rows,
ch 2; working across sts on Row 171, 2 sc in first sc, sc in each
sc across to last sc, 2 sc in last sc, ch 2; join with slip st to first
sc: 660 sc and 4 ch-2 sps.
Rnd 2: Ch 1, sc in same st and in each sc across to next corner
ch-2 sp, (sc, ch 2, sc) in corner ch-2 sp, ★ sc in each sc across
to next corner ch-2 sp, (sc, ch 2, sc) in corner ch-2 sp; repeat
from ★ 2 times **more**; join with slip st to first sc: 668 sc and
4 ch-2 sps.
Rnd 3: Ch 1, skip next sc, † (dc, ch 1, dc) in next sc, ch 1, skip
next sc, slip st in next sc, ch 1, skip next sc †, repeat from
† to † across to next corner ch-2 sp, (dc, ch 1) 4 times in
corner ch-2 sp, skip next sc, ★ slip st in next sc, ch 1, skip next
sc, repeat from † to † across to next corner ch-2 sp, (dc, ch 1)
4 times in corner ch-2 sp, skip next sc; repeat from ★ 2 times
more; join with slip st to joining slip st, do **not** finish off:
344 dc and 512 ch-1 sps.

Continued on page 61.

ENGAGING PATTERN

A medley of stitches create the engaging pattern on this stylish wrap.
Crocheted in a restful hue, the afghan is worked in rows across its length.

Finished Size: 45" x 60½"

MATERIALS
Worsted Weight Yarn:
    53 ounces, (1,510 grams, 3,635 yards)
Crochet hook, size H (5.00 mm) **or** size needed
    for gauge

GAUGE: 15 sc = 4"; Rows 4-13 = 3½"

Gauge Swatch: 5"w x 3½"h
Ch 20 **loosely**.
Work same as Afghan Body for 10 rows.
Finish off.

Each row is worked across length of Afghan.

STITCH GUIDE

> **BACK POST DOUBLE CROCHET (abbreviated BPdc)**
> YO, insert hook from **back** to **front** around post of st indicated *(Fig. 13, page 141)*, YO and pull up a loop, (YO and draw through 2 loops on hook) twice. Skip st in front of BPdc.
>
> **FRONT POST DOUBLE CROCHET**
>   **(abbreviated FPdc)**
> YO, insert hook from **front** to **back** around post of st indicated *(Fig. 11, page 140)*, YO and pull up a loop, (YO and draw through 2 loops on hook) twice.
>
> **FRONT POST DOUBLE CROCHET CLUSTER**
>   **(abbreviated FPdc Cluster)** (uses 2 tr)
> YO, insert hook from **front** to **back** around post of tr just worked into *(Fig. 10, page 140)*, YO and pull up a loop, YO and draw through 2 loops on hook, skip next dc, YO, insert hook from **front** to **back** around post of next tr, YO and pull up a loop, YO and draw through 2 loops on hook, YO and draw through all 3 loops on hook.

> **FLOWER**
> Ch 1, rotate piece clockwise holding beginning ch away from you, working in free loop of same ch as last slip st *(Fig. 21b, page 142)*, † ★ (YO, insert hook in same ch, YO and pull up a loop) 4 times, YO and draw through all 9 loops on hook, ch 1, slip st in same ch, ch 1; repeat from ★ once **more** †, rotate piece clockwise holding beginning ch toward you, repeat from † to † once working around first slip st made.
> **TR CLUSTER**
> YO twice, insert hook in last FPdc Cluster worked into, YO and pull up a loop, (YO and draw through 2 loops on hook) twice, YO twice, skip next Flower and next sc, insert hook in next st, YO and pull up a loop, (YO and draw through 2 loops on hook) twice, YO and draw through all 3 loops on hook.

AFGHAN BODY

Ch 228 **loosely**.

Row 1 (Right side)**:** Sc in second ch from hook and in each ch across: 227 sc.

Note: Loop a short piece of yarn around any stitch to mark Row 1 as **right** side.

Row 2: Ch 1, turn; sc in each sc across.

Row 3: Ch 3 **(counts as first dc, now and throughout)**, turn; dc in next sc and in each sc across.

Row 4: Ch 1, turn; sc in first dc, (work BPdc around next dc, sc in next dc) across.

Row 5: Ch 1, turn; sc in first sc, (work FPdc around next BPdc, sc in next sc) across.

Rows 6 and 7: Ch 1, turn; sc in each st across.

Row 8: Ch 3, turn; ★ dc in next sc, skip next 3 sc, (tr, ch 5, tr) in next sc, skip next 3 sc; repeat from ★ across to last 2 sc, dc in last 2 sc: 87 sts and 28 ch-5 sps.

Row 9: Ch 1, turn; sc in first 2 dc, work FPdc around next tr, sc in same tr as last FPdc, slip st in next 3 chs, work Flower, slip st in next 2 chs, sc in next tr, ★ work FPdc Cluster, sc in same tr as last leg of FPdc Cluster, slip st in next 3 chs, work Flower, slip st in next 2 chs, sc in next tr; repeat from ★ across to last 2 dc, work FPdc around last tr worked into, sc in last 2 dc, do **not** finish off: 28 Flowers.

Continued on page 61.

...bouquet of playful violets to any room with this mile-a-minute beauty! Crafted using the join-as-you-go method, the vibrant afghan is brightened with flowers in every other diamond-shaped motif.

Finished Size: 49" x 64"

MATERIALS
Worsted Weight Yarn:
Ecru - 28 ounces, (800 grams, 1,585 yards)
Green - 17$\frac{1}{2}$ ounces, (500 grams, 990 yards)
Purple - 7 ounces, (200 grams, 395 yards)
Yellow - 3$\frac{1}{2}$ ounces, (100 grams, 200 yards)
Crochet hook, size G (4.00 mm) **or** size needed for gauge

GAUGE: Each Strip = 3$\frac{3}{4}$" wide

Gauge Swatch: 2" square
Work same as First Motif.

STITCH GUIDE

DC CLUSTER
† YO, insert hook in **next** sp, YO and pull up a loop, YO and draw through 2 loops on hook †, YO, insert hook in side of joining sc, YO and pull up a loop, YO and draw through 2 loops on hook, repeat from † to † once, YO and draw through all 4 loops on hook **(counts as one dc)**.
TR CLUSTER (uses next 5 dc)
★ YO twice, insert hook in **next** dc, YO and pull up a loop, (YO and draw through 2 loops on hook) twice; repeat from ★ 4 times **more**, YO and draw through all 6 loops on hook *(Figs. 16a & b, page 141)*.

STRIP A (Make 7)
FIRST MOTIF
Rnd 1 (Right side): With Yellow, ch 2, 8 sc in second ch from hook; join with slip st to first sc, finish off.
Note: Loop a short piece of yarn around any stitch to mark Rnd 1 as **right** side.
Rnd 2: With **right** side facing and working in Front Loops Only *(Fig. 20, page 142)*, join Purple with sc in any sc *(see Joining With Sc, page 142)*; ch 5, sc in same st, (sc, ch 5, sc) in each sc around; join with slip st to **both** loops of first sc, finish off: 8 petals.

Rnd 3: With **right** side facing, working **behind** Rnd 2 and working free loops of sc on Rnd 1 *(Fig. 21a, page 142)*, join Green with sc in any sc; ch 3, (sc in next sc, ch 3) around; join with slip st to first sc, do **not** finish off: 8 ch-3 sps.
Rnd 4: Slip st in first ch-3 sp, ch 1, sc in same sp, (2 hdc, ch 3, 2 hdc) in next ch-3 sp, ★ sc in next ch-3 sp, (2 hdc, ch 3, 2 hdc) in next ch-3 sp; repeat from ★ 2 times **more**; join with slip st to first sc, finish off: 20 sts and 4 ch-3 sps.

SECOND MOTIF
Rnd 1 (Right side): With Green, ch 2, 8 sc in second ch from hook; join with slip st to first sc.
Note: Mark Rnd 1 as **right** side.
Rnd 2: Ch 1, sc in same st, ch 3, (sc in next sc, ch 3) around; join with slip st to first sc: 8 ch-3 sps.
Rnd 3 (Joining rnd): Slip st in first ch-3 sp, ch 1, sc in same sp, ★ (2 hdc, ch 3, 2 hdc) in next ch-3 sp, sc in next ch-3 sp; repeat from ★ 2 times **more**, 2 hdc in last ch-3 sp, ch 1, holding Motifs with **wrong** sides together, sc in corresponding corner ch-3 sp on **previous** Motif *(Fig. 24, page 143)*, ch 1, 2 hdc in same sp on **new** Motif; join with slip st to first sc, finish off.

THIRD MOTIF
Rnds 1-3: Work same as First Motif: 8 ch-3 sps.
Rnd 4 (Joining rnd): Slip st in first ch-3 sp, ch 1, sc in same sp, ★ (2 hdc, ch 3, 2 hdc) in next ch-3 sp, sc in next ch-3 sp; repeat from ★ 2 times **more**, 2 hdc in last ch-3 sp, ch 1, holding Motifs with **wrong** sides together, sc in corresponding corner ch-3 sp on **previous** Motif, ch 1, 2 hdc in same sp on **new** Motif; join with slip st to first sc, finish off.

REMAINING 16 MOTIFS
Repeat Second and Third Motifs, 8 times.

Continued on page 60.

STRIP B (Make 6)

FIRST MOTIF

Rnd 1 (Right side): With Green, ch 2, 8 sc in second ch from hook; join with slip st to first sc.

Note: Mark Rnd 1 as **right** side.

Rnd 2: Ch 1, sc in same st, ch 3, (sc in next sc, ch 3) around; join with slip st to first sc: 8 ch-3 sps.

Rnd 3: Slip st in first ch-3 sp, ch 1, sc in same sp, (2 hdc, ch 3, 2 hdc) in next ch-3 sp, ★ sc in next ch-3 sp, (2 hdc, ch 3, 2 hdc) in next ch-3 sp; repeat from ★ 2 times **more**; join with slip st to first sc, finish off: 20 sts and 4 ch-3 sps.

SECOND MOTIF

Rnd 1 (Right side): With Yellow, ch 2, 8 sc in second ch from hook; join with slip st to first sc, finish off.

Note: Mark Rnd 1 as **right** side.

Rnd 2: With **right** side facing and working in Front Loops Only, join Purple with sc in any sc; ch 5, sc in same st, (sc, ch 5, sc) in each sc around; join with slip st to **both** loops of first sc, finish off: 8 petals.

Rnd 3: With **right** side facing, working **behind** Rnd 2 and in free loops of sc on Rnd 1, join Green with sc in any sc; ch 3, (sc in next sc, ch 3) around; join with slip st to first sc, do **not** finish off: 8 ch-3 sps.

Rnd 4 (Joining rnd): Slip st in first ch-3 sp, ch 1, sc in same sp, ★ (2 hdc, ch 3, 2 hdc) in next ch-3 sp, sc in next ch-3 sp; repeat from ★ 2 times **more**, 2 hdc in last ch-3 sp, ch 1, holding Motifs with **wrong** sides together, sc in corresponding corner ch-3 sp on **previous Motif**, ch 1, 2 hdc in same sp on **new Motif**; join with slip st to first sc, finish off.

THIRD MOTIF

Rnds 1 and 2: Work same as First Motif: 8 ch-3 sps.

Rnd 3 (Joining rnd): Slip st in first ch-3 sp, ch 1, sc in same sp, ★ (2 hdc, ch 3, 2 hdc) in next ch-3 sp, sc in next ch-3 sp; repeat from ★ 2 times **more**, 2 hdc in last ch-3 sp, ch 1, holding Motifs with **wrong** sides together, sc in corresponding corner ch-3 sp on **previous Motif**, ch 1, 2 hdc in same sp on **new Motif**; join with slip st to first sc, finish off.

REMAINING 16 MOTIFS

Repeat Second and Third Motifs, 8 times.

EDGING

Beginning and ending with Strip A, alternately add Edging to Strips A and B for assembly.

FIRST STRIP

Rnd 1: With **right** side facing, join Ecru with sc in end ch-3 sp; 2 sc in same sp, sc in next 5 sts, 3 sc in next ch-3 sp, † sc in next hdc, hdc in next hdc, dc in next 3 sts, work dc Cluster, dc in next 3 sts, hdc in next hdc, sc in next hdc, 3 sc in next ch-3 sp †, repeat from † to † 17 times **more**, (sc in next 5 sts, 3 sc in next ch-3 sp) twice, repeat from † to † across to last 5 sts, sc in last 5 sts; join with slip st to first sc: 536 sts.

Rnd 2: Ch 1, (sc, ch 3, sc) in same st, † ch 5, (sc, ch 7, sc) in next sc, ch 5, (sc, ch 3, sc) in next sc, (ch 3, sc in next sc) 6 times, (sc, ch 3, sc) in next sc, ★ sc in next sc, hdc in next sc, dc in next hdc, ch 3, tr in next dc, ch 1, work tr Cluster, ch 1, tr in next dc, ch 3, dc in next hdc, hdc in next sc, sc in next sc, (sc, ch 3, sc) in next sc; repeat from ★ 17 times **more**, (sc in next sc, ch 3) 6 times †, (sc, ch 3, sc) in next sc, repeat from † to † once; join with slip st to first sc, finish off: 436 sts and 216 sps.

REMAINING 12 STRIPS

Rnd 1: Work same as First Strip: 536 sts.

Rnd 2 (Joining rnd): Ch 1, (sc, ch 3, sc) in same st, ch 5, (sc, ch 7, sc) in next sc, ch 5, (sc, ch 3, sc) in next sc, (ch 3, sc in next sc) 6 times, (sc, ch 3, sc) in next sc, ★ sc in next sc, hdc in next sc, dc in next hdc, ch 3, tr in next dc, ch 1, work tr Cluster, ch 1, tr in next dc, ch 3, dc in next hdc, hdc in next sc, sc in next sc, (sc ch 3, sc) in next sc; repeat from ★ 17 times **more**, (sc in next sc, ch 3) 6 times, (sc, ch 3, sc) in next sc, ch 5, (sc, ch 7, sc) in next sc, ch 5, (sc, ch 3) twice in next sc, (sc in next sc, ch 3) 5 times, sc in next 2 sc, ch 1; holding Strips with **wrong** sides together, sc in corresponding ch-3 sp on **previous Strip**, ch 1, † sc in same st and in next sc on **new Strip**, hdc in next sc, dc in next hdc, ch 1, sc in next ch-3 sp on **previous Strip**, ch 1, tr in next dc on **new Strip**, ch 1, work tr Cluster, ch 1, tr in next dc, ch 1, sc in next ch-3 sp on **previous Strip**, ch 1, dc in next hdc on **new Strip**, hdc in next sc, sc in next 2 sc, ch 1, sc in next ch-3 sp on **previous Strip**, ch 1 †, repeat from † to † 17 times **more**, sc in same st on **new Strip**, (sc in next sc, ch 3) 6 times; join with slip st to first sc, finish off.

FLOWERS FOR BABY Continued from page 52.

Rnd 2: Ch 1, **turn**; slip st in first ch-1 sp, ch 4, ★ (dc in next ch-1 sp, ch 1) across to next corner ch-3 sp, (dc, ch 3, dc) in corner ch-3 sp, ch 1; repeat from ★ around; join with slip st to first dc: 328 dc and 4 ch-3 sps.

Rnd 3: Ch 5 **(counts as first dc plus ch 2, now and throughout)**, do **not** turn; dc in same st, ch 2, ★ (dc, ch 2) twice in each dc across to next corner ch-3 sp, (dc, ch 2) 4 times in corner ch-3 sp; repeat from ★ 3 times **more**, (dc, ch 2) twice in last dc; join with slip st to first dc.

Rnd 4: (Slip st in next ch-2 sp, ch 3) around; join with slip st to first slip st, finish off.

RUFFLE

Rnd 1: With **right** side facing, working in **front** of Edging and in sc and corner ch-3 sps on Rnd 1 of Edging, join White with slip st in any corner ch-3 sp (between dc); ch 5, dc in same sp, ch 2, ★ (dc, ch 2) twice in each sc across to next corner ch-3 sp, (dc, ch 2) twice in corner ch-3 sp (between dc); repeat from ★ 2 times **more**, (dc, ch 2) twice in each sc across; join with slip st to first dc.

Rnd 2: (Slip st in next ch-2 sp, ch 3) around; join with slip st to first slip st, finish off.

SPIDER LACE Continued from page 54.

Rnd 4: Slip st in next ch, slip st in next dc and in next ch-1 sp, ch 3 **(counts as first dc)**, 2 dc in same sp, ch 1, skip next 2 ch-1 sps, (3 dc in next ch-1 sp, ch 1, skip next 2 ch-1 sps) 42 times, † (3 dc in next ch-1 sp, ch 1) 3 times, skip next 2 ch-1 sps, (3 dc in next ch-1 sp, ch 1, skip next 2 ch-1 sps) 39 times, (3 dc in next ch-1 sp, ch 1) 3 times, skip next 2 ch-1 sps †, (3 dc in next ch-1 sp, ch 1, skip next 2 ch-1 sps) 43 times, repeat from † to † once; join with slip st to first dc: 528 dc.

Rnd 5: Slip st in next dc, ch 4, dc in same st, ch 1, slip st in next ch-1 sp, ch 1, skip next dc, ★ (dc, ch 1) twice in next dc, slip st in next ch-1 sp, ch 1, skip next st; repeat from ★ around; join with slip st to third ch of beginning ch-4, finish off.

ENGAGING PATTERN Continued from page 56.

Row 10: Ch 3, turn; working in **front** of and to right of next sc, tr in same st as sc worked into, ch 3, YO twice, skip next sc, insert hook in next FPdc, YO and pull up a loop, (YO and draw through 2 loops on hook) twice, YO twice, working in **front** of next Flower, skip Flower and next sc, insert hook in next FPdc Cluster, YO and pull up a loop, (YO and draw through 2 loops on hook) twice, YO and draw through all 3 loops on hook, ch 3, ★ working in **front** of same FPdc Cluster just worked into, tr in skipped dc one row **below** FPdc Cluster, ch 3, work tr Cluster, ch 3; repeat from ★ across to last 2 sc, working in **front** of and to left of next sc, tr in same st as sc worked into, dc in last sc: 59 sts and 56 ch-3 sps.

Row 11: Ch 1, turn; sc in each st and in each ch across: 227 sc.

Row 12: Ch 1, turn; sc in each sc across.

Row 13: Ch 3, turn; dc in next sc and in each sc across.

Rows 14-127: Repeat Rows 4-13, 11 times; then repeat Rows 4-7 once **more**; do **not** finish off.

EDGING

Ch 1, do **not** turn; 2 sc in top of last sc made on Row 127; sc evenly across end of rows; working in free loops of beginning ch, 3 sc in first ch, sc in next 225 chs, 3 sc in next ch; sc evenly across end of rows; working in sts across Row 127, 3 sc in first sc, sc in next sc and in each sc across, sc in same st as first sc; join with slip st to first sc, finish off.

Using photo as a guide for placement and holding 10 strands of yarn together, each 17" long, add fringe evenly across short edges of Afghan *(Figs. 27b & d, page 143)*.

GARDEN ROMANCE

Soft garden tones blend harmoniously in this rippled wrap for a touch of romance. A generous fringe of dark green adds to its lushness.

JUNE

STITCH GUIDE

BEGINNING DECREASE (uses next 2 dc)
★ YO, insert hook in **next** dc, YO and pull up a loop, YO and draw through 2 loops on hook; repeat from ★ once **more**, YO and draw through all 3 loops on hook (**counts as one dc**).
SPLIT DECREASE (uses next 5 sts and next 2 ch-2 sps)
† YO, insert hook in **next** dc, YO and pull up a loop, YO and draw through 2 loops on hook †; repeat from † to † once **more**, skip next 2 ch-2 sps, repeat from † to † twice, YO and draw through all 5 loops on hook (**counts as one dc**).
ENDING DECREASE (uses last 3 sts and last ch-2 sp)
† YO, insert hook in **next** st, YO and pull up a loop, YO and draw through 2 loops on hook †; repeat from † to † once **more**, skip last ch-2 sp, repeat from † to † once, YO and draw through all 4 loops on hook (**counts as one dc**).

COLOR SEQUENCE
2 Rows Green (**Fig. 22a, page 142**), ★ 2 rows **each**: Pink, Ecru, Lt Green, Green; repeat from ★ 11 times **more**.

Finished Size: 46" x 63"

MATERIALS
Worsted Weight Yarn:
    Green - 16½ ounces,
        (470 grams, 1,130 yards)
    Lt Green - 10½ ounces,
        (300 grams, 720 yards)
    Pink - 10 ounces,
        (280 grams, 685 yards)
    Ecru - 10 ounces,
        (280 grams, 685 yards)
Crochet hook, size H (5.00 mm) **or** size needed for gauge

GAUGE: In pattern, 2 repeats = 5";
        7 rows = 4½ "

Gauge Swatch: 5¼ "w x 4½ "h
With Green, ch 22 **loosely**.
Work same as Afghan Body for 7 rows.
Finish off.

AFGHAN BODY
With Green, ch 182 **loosely**.
Row 1 (Right side): Sc in second ch from hook, ★ ch 2, skip next 4 chs, (2 dc, ch 2) 3 times in next ch, skip next 4 chs, sc in next ch; repeat from ★ across: 108 dc, 19 sc, and 72 ch-2 sps.
Note: Loop a short piece of yarn around any stitch to mark Row 1 as **right** side.
Row 2: Ch 2, turn; work beginning decrease, ch 2, (2 dc, ch 2, dc) in next dc, (dc, ch 2, 2 dc) in next dc, ch 2, ★ work Split decrease, ch 2, (2 dc, ch 2, dc) in next dc, (dc, ch 2, 2 dc) in next dc, ch 2; repeat from ★ across to last 2 ch-2 sps, skip next ch-2 sp, work ending decrease changing to next color: 127 dc.
Row 3: Ch 2, turn; work beginning decrease, ch 2, (2 dc, ch 2, dc) in next dc, (dc, ch 2, 2 dc) in next dc, ch 2, ★ work Split decrease, ch 2, (2 dc, ch 2, dc) in next dc, (dc, ch 2, 2 dc) in next dc, ch 2; repeat from ★ across to last 2 ch-2 sps, skip next ch-2 sp, work ending decrease.
Rows 4-98: Repeat Rows 2 and 3, 47 times; then repeat Row 2 once **more**; at end of Row 98, do **not** change colors, do **not** finish off.

Continued on page 76.

GRACEFUL SHELLS

Decorative shells grace this fanciful afghan, which is ideal for wrapping up in on a breezy evening. The mile-a-minute beauty is worked in a rosy hue reminiscent of a summer sunset.

Finished Size: 45" x 63"

MATERIALS
Worsted Weight Yarn:
39 ounces, (1,110 grams, 2,205 yards)
Crochet hook, size I (5.50 mm) **or** size needed for gauge

GAUGE: Each Strip = 7¹/₂ " wide

Gauge Swatch: 5¹/₂ "w x 6"h
Work same as Center through Row 7.

FIRST STRIP
CENTER
Ch 24 **loosely**, place marker in fourth ch from hook for st placement.
Row 1 (Right side): 7 Dc in ninth ch from hook, ch 1, skip next 4 chs, dc in next ch, ch 1, skip next 4 chs, 7 dc in next ch, ch 1, skip next 4 chs, dc in last ch: 4 sps.
Note: Loop a short piece of yarn around any stitch to mark Row 1 as **right** side and bottom edge.
Row 2: Ch 4 **(counts as first dc plus ch 1, now and throughout)**, turn; dc in same st, ch 1, skip next 2 dc, dc in next 3 dc, ch 1, skip next 2 dc, (dc, ch 3, dc) in next dc, ch 1, skip next 2 dc, dc in next 3 dc, ch 1, skip next 2 dc and next ch, (dc, ch 1, dc) in next ch: 12 dc and 7 sps.
Row 3: Ch 3 **(counts as first dc, now and throughout)**, turn; 3 dc in next ch-1 sp, ch 1, skip next 2 dc, dc in next dc, ch 1, skip next ch-1 sp, 7 dc in next ch-3 sp, ch 1, skip next 2 dc, dc in next dc, ch 1, skip next ch-1 sp, 3 dc in next ch-1 sp, dc in last dc: 17 dc and 4 ch-1 sps.
Row 4: Ch 3, turn; dc in next dc, ch 1, skip next dc, (dc, ch 3, dc) in next dc, ch 1, skip next 3 dc, dc in next 3 dc, ch 1, skip next 3 dc, (dc, ch 3, dc) in next dc, ch 1, skip next dc, dc in last 2 dc: 11 dc and 6 sps.
Row 5: Ch 4, turn; skip next ch-1 sp, 7 dc in next ch-3 sp, ch 1, skip next 2 dc, dc in next dc, ch 1, skip next ch-1 sp, 7 dc in next ch-3 sp, ch 1, skip next 2 dc, dc in last dc: 17 dc and 4 ch-1 sps.
Row 6: Ch 4, turn; dc in same st, ch 1, skip next 2 dc, dc in next 3 dc, ch 1, skip next 2 dc, (dc, ch 3, dc) in next dc, ch 1, skip next 2 dc, dc in next 3 dc, ch 1, skip next 2 dc, (dc, ch 1, dc) in last dc: 12 dc and 7 sps.

Rows 7-77: Repeat Rows 3-6, 17 times; then repeat Rows 3-5 once **more**.
Row 78: Ch 7 **(counts as first dc plus ch 4)**, turn; skip next 3 dc, sc in next dc, ch 4, skip next 3 dc, hdc in next dc, ch 4, skip next 3 dc, sc in next dc, ch 4, skip next 3 dc, dc in last dc; do **not** finish off: 5 sts and 4 ch-4 sps.

EDGING
Rnd 1: Ch 1, turn; sc in each st and in each ch across to last dc, 2 sc in last dc; 2 sc in first row, 3 sc in end of each row across; working in free loops of beginning ch *(Fig. 21b, page 142)*, 2 sc in first ch, sc in each ch across to marked ch, 2 sc in marked ch, remove marker; 2 sc in first row, 3 sc in end of each row across, sc in same st as first sc; join with slip st to first sc: 512 sc.
Rnd 2: Slip st in next sc, ch 1, sc in same st, skip next sc, (hdc, ch 3, hdc) in next sc, skip next sc, ★ sc in next sc, skip next sc, (hdc, ch 3, hdc) in next sc, skip next st; repeat from ★ around; join with slip st to first sc: 128 ch-3 sps.
Rnd 3: Slip st in next hdc and in next ch-3 sp, ch 1, (sc, ch 3) twice in same sp and in next 63 ch-3 sps, place marker around last ch-3 made for joining placement, (sc, ch 3) twice in each ch-3 sp around; join with slip st to first sc, finish off.

REMAINING 5 STRIPS
Work same as First Strip through Rnd 2 of Edging: 128 ch-3 sps.
Rnd 3 (Joining rnd): Slip st in next hdc and in next ch-3 sp, ch 1, (sc, ch 3) twice in same sp and in next 63 ch-3 sps, place marker around last ch-3 made for joining placement, (sc, ch 3) twice in next 4 ch-3 sps, sc in next ch-3 sp, ch 1; holding Strips with **wrong** sides together and bottom edges at same end, slip st in marked ch-3 sp on **previous Strip** *(Fig. 24, page 143)*, ch 1, sc in same sp on **new Strip**, ch 3, ★ sc in next ch-3 sp, ch 1, slip st in next ch-3 sp on **previous Strip**, ch 1, sc in same sp on **new Strip**, ch 3; repeat from ★ 58 times **more**; join with slip st to first sc, finish off.

Holding 6 strands of yarn together, each 18" long, add fringe in every other ch-3 sp across short edges of Afghan *(Figs. 27a & c, page 143)*.

SUMMER STYLE

*Light and airy in white, this lacy throw has a carefree style
that's just right for summer! Though it features a distinctive pattern
of alternating panels, it's actually worked in rows across its length.*

Finished Size: 48" x 66"

MATERIALS
Worsted Weight Yarn:
41 ounces, (1,160 grams, 2,655 yards)
Crochet hook, size H (5.00 mm) **or** size needed
for gauge

GAUGE: In pattern, 13 sts = 3"; 8 rows = 3½"

Gauge Swatch: 3¼"w x 3½"h
Ch 17 **loosely**.
Work same as Afghan Body for 8 rows.
Finish off.

Each row is worked across length of Afghan.

AFGHAN BODY
Ch 281 **loosely**.
Row 1 (Right side)**:** Dc in fourth ch from hook **(3 skipped
chs count as first dc)** and in next ch, ★ ch 1, skip next ch, dc
in next 3 chs; repeat from ★ across: 210 dc and 69 ch-1 sps.
Note: Loop a short piece of yarn around any stitch to mark
Row 1 as **right** side.
Row 2: Ch 4 **(counts as first dc plus ch 1, now and
throughout)**, turn; skip next dc, dc in next dc, ★ dc in next
ch-1 sp and in next dc, ch 1, skip next dc, dc in next dc; repeat
from ★ across: 209 dc and 70 ch-1 sps.
Row 3: Ch 3 **(counts as first dc, now and throughout)**,
turn; dc in next ch-1 sp and in next dc, ★ ch 1, skip next dc, dc
in next dc, dc in next ch-1 sp and in next dc; repeat from ★
across: 210 dc and 69 ch-1 sps.
Row 4: Ch 4, turn; skip next dc, dc in next dc, ★ dc in next
ch-1 sp and in next dc, ch 1, skip next dc, dc in next dc; repeat
from ★ across: 209 dc and 70 ch-1 sps.
Row 5: Ch 3, turn; dc in next ch-1 sp and in next dc, ★ ch 1,
skip next dc, dc in next dc, dc in next ch-1 sp and in next dc;
repeat from ★ across: 210 dc and 69 ch-1 sps.
Row 6: Ch 4, turn; ★ skip next dc, (dc in next dc, ch 1) twice;
repeat from ★ across to last 2 dc, skip next dc, dc in last dc:
140 dc and 139 ch-1 sps.

Row 7: Ch 3, turn; dc in next ch-1 sp and in each dc and each
ch-1 sp across: 279 dc.
Row 8: Ch 4, turn; skip next dc, dc in next dc, ★ ch 1, skip
next dc, dc in next dc; repeat from ★ across: 140 dc and
139 ch-1 sps.
Row 9: Ch 4, turn; dc in next dc, (ch 1, dc in next dc) 4 times,
dc in next ch-1 sp and in next dc, ★ (ch 1, dc in next dc) 7
times, dc in next ch-1 sp and in next dc; repeat from ★ across
to last 5 dc, (ch 1, dc in next dc) 5 times: 157 dc and
122 ch-1 sps.
Row 10: Ch 4, turn; dc in next dc, (ch 1, dc in next dc) 3
times, dc in next ch-1 sp and in next dc, ch 5, skip next dc,
in next dc, dc in next ch-1 sp and in next dc, ★ (ch 1, dc in
next dc) 5 times, dc in next ch-1 sp and in next dc, ch 5, skip
next dc, dc in next dc, dc in next ch-1 sp and in next dc; repeat
from ★ across to last 4 dc, (ch 1, dc in next dc) 4 times:
174 dc and 105 sps.
Row 11: Ch 4, turn; dc in next dc, (ch 1, dc in next dc) twice,
★ dc in next ch-1 sp and in next dc, ch 4, sc in next ch-5 sp,
ch 4, skip next 2 dc, dc in next dc, dc in next ch-1 sp and in
next dc, (ch 1, dc in next dc) 3 times; repeat from ★ across:
140 dc.
Row 12: Ch 4, turn; dc in next dc, ★ ch 1, dc in next dc, dc in
next ch-1 sp and in next dc, ch 4, skip next 2 dc and next
3 chs, sc in next ch, sc in next sc and in next ch, ch 4, skip next
2 dc, dc in next dc, dc in next ch-1 sp and in next dc; repeat
from ★ across to last 2 dc, (ch 1, dc in next dc) twice: 106 dc.
Row 13: Ch 4, turn; dc in next dc, dc in next ch-1 sp and in
next dc, ★ ch 4, skip next 2 dc and next 3 chs, sc in next ch, sc
in next 3 sc and in next ch, ch 4, skip next 2 dc, dc in next dc,
dc in next ch-1 sp and in next dc; repeat from ★ across to last
dc, ch 1, dc in last dc: 56 dc.
Row 14: Ch 4, turn; dc in next dc, ch 1, ★ skip next dc, dc in
next dc and in next 2 chs, ch 4, skip next sc, sc in next 3 sc,
ch 4, skip next sc and next 2 chs, dc in next 2 chs and in next
dc, ch 1; repeat from ★ across to last 3 dc, skip next dc, dc in
next dc, ch 1, dc in last dc; do **not** finish off: 106 dc.

Continued on page 76.

ROSY WRAP

Beautifully textured roses blossom on the panels of this granny-style afghan. It's perfect for adding a feminine style to any setting. A scalloped border completes the wrap.

Finished Size: 52½" x 68½"

MATERIALS

Worsted Weight Yarn:
   Ecru - 29 ounces, (820 grams, 1,990 yards)
   Lt Rose - 16 ounces, (450 grams, 1,095 yards)
   Green - 15 ounces, (430 grams, 1,030 yards)
   Rose - 13 ounces, (370 grams, 890 yards)
Crochet hook, size G (4.00 mm) **or** size needed
   for gauge
Yarn needle

GAUGE: Each Square = 8"

Gauge Swatch: 4"
Work same as First Square through Rnd 8.

STITCH GUIDE

> **JOINING SQUARES**
> Drop loop from hook, with **right** side of **previous Square** facing, insert hook from **front** to **back** in corresponding dc, hook dropped loop and draw through.
>
> **CLUSTER** (uses next 4 sts)
> ★ YO twice, insert hook in **next** st, YO and pull up a loop, (YO and draw through 2 loops on hook) twice; repeat from ★ 3 times **more**, YO and draw through all 5 loops on hook *(Figs. 16a & b, page 141)*.
>
> **JOINING CLUSTER**
> † YO twice, insert hook in **next** dc, YO and pull up a loop, (YO and draw through 2 loops on hook) twice †; repeat from † to † once **more**, skip next joining, repeat from † to † twice, YO and draw through all 5 loops on hook.

PANEL (Make 5)
FIRST SQUARE

With Rose, ch 5; join with slip st to form a ring.

Rnd 1 (Right side)**:** Ch 5 **(counts as first dc plus ch 2)**, (dc in ring, ch 2) 7 times; join with slip st to first dc: 8 dc and 8 ch-2 sps.

Note: Loop a short piece of yarn around any stitch to mark Rnd 1 as **right** side.

Rnd 2: Ch 1, (sc, hdc, dc, hdc, sc) around post of each dc around; join with slip st to first sc, finish off: 8 petals.

Rnd 3: With **right** side facing and working **behind** petals, join Lt Rose with slip st in any ch-2 sp on Rnd 1; ch 1, (sc, hdc, 3 dc, hdc, sc) in same sp and in each ch-2 sp around; join with slip st to first sc changing to Rose *(Fig. 22b, page 142)*: 8 petals.

Rnd 4: Ch 3, working **behind** petals, (slip st in sp **between** next 2 sc, ch 3) around *(Fig. 23, page 143)*; join with slip st at base of beginning ch-3: 8 ch-3 sps.

Rnd 5: Slip st in first ch-3 sp, ch 1, (sc, hdc, 4 dc, hdc, sc) in same sp and in each ch-3 sp around; join with slip st to first sc changing to Lt Rose: 8 petals.

Rnd 6: Ch 4, working **behind** petals, (slip st in sp **between** next 2 sc, ch 4) around; join with slip st at base of beginning ch-4: 8 ch-4 sps.

Rnd 7: Slip st in first ch-4 sp, ch 1, (sc, hdc, 5 dc, hdc, sc) in same sp and in each ch-4 sp around; join with slip st to first sc, finish off: 8 petals.

Rnd 8: With **right** side facing and working in Back Loops Only *(Fig. 20, page 142)*, skip first 3 sts of first petal and join Green with slip st in next dc; ch 1, sc in same st and in next 2 dc, ch 3, (3 dc, ch 2, 3 dc) in center dc of next petal, ch 3, skip next 7 sts, ★ sc in next 3 dc, ch 3, (3 dc, ch 2, 3 dc) in center dc of next petal, ch 3, skip next 7 sts; repeat from ★ 2 times **more**; join with slip st to **both** loops of first sc, finish off: 12 sps.

Rnd 9: With **right** side facing and working in both loops, join Ecru with slip st in center sc of any 3-sc group; ch 3 **(counts as first dc, now and throughout)**, 2 dc in same st, 5 dc in next ch-3 sp, (3 dc, ch 2, 3 dc) in next ch-2 sp, 5 dc in next ch-3 sp, ★ 3 dc in center sc of next 3-sc group, 5 dc in next ch-3 sp, (3 dc, ch 2, 3 dc) in next ch-2 sp, 5 dc in next ch-3 sp; repeat from ★ 2 times **more**; join with slip st to first dc, finish off: 76 dc and 4 ch-2 sps.

Continued on page 77.

FIELD OF DAISIES

If you count daisies among your favorite things, you'll want to pick this comforter for your next project! It sports a field of cheery white flowers with yellow faces against a soft field of green.

Finished Size: 54" x 76"

MATERIALS

Worsted Weight Yarn:
 Green - 48½ ounces, (1,380 grams, 3,325 yards)
 White - 11 ounces, (310 grams, 755 yards)
 Yellow - 4 ounces, (110 grams, 275 yards)
Crochet hook, size I (5.50 mm) **or** size needed
 for gauge

GAUGE: Each Motif = 8" diameter

Gauge Swatch: 5½ " diameter
Work same as First Motif through Rnd 7.

STITCH GUIDE

PETAL
Ch 9 **loosely**, working in back ridges of chs *(Fig. 2b, page 139)*, slip st in second ch from hook, hdc in next ch, dc in next 5 chs, slip st in last ch.

JOINING SC
Insert hook in unworked ch at tip of nearest Petal and in st indicated, YO and draw through st and Petal, YO and draw through both loops on hook **(counts as one sc)**.

PICOT
Ch 5, sc in third ch from hook, ch 2.

MOTIFS

FIRST AND SECOND

With Yellow, ch 4; join with slip st to form a ring.
Rnd 1 (Right side)**:** Ch 2, 10 hdc in ring; join with slip st to Back Loop Only of first hdc *(Fig. 20, page 142)*: 10 hdc.
Note: Loop a short piece of yarn around any stitch to mark Rnd 1 as **right** side.
Rnd 2: Ch 1, sc in same st, ch 4, skip next hdc, ★ sc in Back Loop Only of next hdc, ch 4, skip next hdc; repeat from ★ around; join with slip st to **both** loops of first sc, finish off: 5 ch-4 sps.
Rnd 3: With **right** side facing, working in Front Loops Only of unworked hdc on Rnd 1 and in free loops of remaining hdc on Rnd 1 *(Fig. 21a, page 142)*, join White with slip st in any hdc; work Petal, (slip st in next hdc, work Petal) around; join with slip st to first slip st, finish off: 10 Petals.
Rnd 4: With **right** side facing, working **behind** Petals and in ch-4 sps on Rnd 2, join Green with slip st in any ch-4 sp; ch 3 **(counts as first dc, now and throughout)**, 5 dc in same sp, 6 dc in each ch-4 sp around; join with slip st to first dc: 30 dc.
Rnd 5: Ch 3, dc in next dc, 2 dc in next dc, ★ dc in next 2 dc, 2 dc in next dc; repeat from ★ around; join with slip st to first dc: 40 dc.
Rnd 6: Ch 3, dc in next 2 dc, 2 dc in next dc, ★ dc in next 3 dc, 2 dc in next dc; repeat from ★ around; join with slip st to first dc: 50 dc.
Rnd 7 (Joining rnd)**:** Ch 1, work joining sc in same st, sc in next 3 dc, 2 sc in next dc, ★ work joining sc in next st, sc in next 3 dc, 2 sc in next dc; repeat from ★ around; join with slip st to first sc: 60 sc.
Rnd 8: Ch 4, skip next sc, ★ hdc in next sc, ch 2, skip next sc; repeat from ★ around; join with slip st to second ch of beginning ch-4: 30 ch-2 sps.
Rnd 9: Slip st in first ch-2 sp, ch 1, 2 sc in same sp, 3 sc in each of next 2 ch-2 sps, ★ 2 sc in next ch-2 sp, 3 sc in each of next 2 ch-2 sps; repeat from ★ around; join with slip st to first sc: 80 sc.
Rnd 10: Ch 1, sc in same st and in next 3 sc, ch 3, (sc in next 4 sc, ch 3) around; join with slip st to first sc, finish off: 20 ch-3 sps.

Continued on page 72.

FIELD OF DAISIES Continued from page 70.

FIELD OF DAISIES Continued from page 70.

Using Placement Diagram as a guide, work Motifs in numerical order, joining as indicated to complete Afghan.

PLACEMENT DIAGRAM

```
59   56   51   44   35
  57   52   45   36
58   53   46   37   26
  54   47   38   27
55   48   39   28   17
  49   40   29   18
50   41   30   19   10
  42   31   20   11
43   32   21   12    5
  33   22   13    6
34   23   14    7    2
  24   15    8    3
25   16    9    4    1
```

THIRD

Work same as First and Second Motifs through Rnd 9: 80 sc.
Rnd 10 (Joining rnd): Ch 1, sc in same st and in next 3 sc, (ch 3, sc in next 4 sc) 12 times, † ch 1, holding Motifs with **wrong** sides together, sc in any ch-3 sp on **adjacent Motif** *(Fig. 24, page 143)*, ch 1, (sc in next 4 sc on **new Motif**, ch 1, sc in next ch-3 sp on **adjacent Motif**, ch 1) twice †, sc in next 4 sc on **new Motif**, (ch 3, sc in next 4 sc) twice, repeat from † to † once; join with slip st to first sc, finish off.

FOURTH

Work same as First and Second Motifs through Rnd 9: 80 sc.
Rnd 10 (Joining rnd): Ch 1, sc in same st and in next 3 sc, (ch 3, sc in next 4 sc) 5 times, place marker around last ch-3 made for joining placement, (ch 3, sc in next 4 sc) 12 times, ch 1, holding Motifs with **wrong** sides together, skip next 2 ch-3 sps from previous joining on **adjacent Motif**, sc in next ch-3 sp, ch 1, (sc in next 4 sc on **new Motif**, ch 1, sc in next ch-3 sp on **adjacent Motif**, ch 1) twice; join with slip st to first sc, finish off.

FIFTH

Work same as First and Second Motifs.

SIXTH

Work same as First and Second Motifs through Rnd 9: 80 sc.
Rnd 10 (Joining rnd): Ch 1, sc in same st and in next 3 sc, (ch 3, sc in next 4 sc) 12 times, ch 1, holding Motifs with **wrong** sides together, skip next 2 ch-3 sps from previous joining on **adjacent Motif**, sc in next ch-3 sp, ch 1, (sc in next 4 sc on **new Motif**, ch 1, sc in next ch-3 sp on **adjacent Motif**, ch 1) twice, sc in next 4 sc on **new Motif**, (ch 3, sc in next 4 sc) twice, ch 1, holding Motifs with **wrong** sides together, sc in any ch-3 sp on **adjacent Motif**, ch 1, (sc in next 4 sc on **new Motif**, ch 1, sc in next ch-3 sp on **adjacent Motif**, ch 1) twice; join with slip st to first sc, finish off.

SEVENTH

Work same as First and Second Motifs through Rnd 9: 80 sc.
Rnd 10 (Joining rnd): Ch 1, sc in same st and in next 3 sc, (ch 3, sc in next 4 sc) 12 times, † ch 1, holding Motifs with **wrong** sides together, skip next 2 ch-3 sps from previous joining on **adjacent Motif**, sc in next ch-3 sp, ch 1, (sc in next 4 sc on **new Motif**, ch 1, sc in next ch-3 sp on **adjacent Motif**, ch 1) twice †, sc in next 4 sc on **new Motif**, (ch 3, sc in next 4 sc) twice, repeat from † to † once; join with slip st to first sc, finish off.

EIGHTH
Work same as First and Second Motifs through Rnd 9: 80 sc.
Rnd 10 (Joining rnd): Ch 1, sc in same st and in next 3 sc,
(ch 3, sc in next 4 sc) 12 times, ch 1, holding Motifs with
wrong sides together, sc in marked ch-3 sp on **adjacent Motif**,
† ch 1, (sc in next 4 sc on **new Motif**, ch 1, sc in next ch-3 sp
on **adjacent Motif**, ch 1) twice †, sc in next 4 sc on **new
Motif**, (ch 3, sc in next 4 sc) twice, ch 1, holding Motifs with
wrong sides together, skip next 2 ch-3 sps from previous
joining on **adjacent Motif**, sc in next ch-3 sp, repeat from
† to † once; join with slip st to first sc, finish off.

NINTH
Work same as Fourth Motif.

10TH
Work same as First and Second Motifs.

11TH
Work same as Sixth Motif.

12TH THROUGH 14TH
Work same as Seventh Motif.

15TH
Work same as Eighth Motif.

16TH
Work same as Fourth Motif.

17TH
Work same as First and Second Motifs.

18TH
Work same as Sixth Motif.

19TH THROUGH 23RD
Work same as Seventh Motif.

24TH
Work same as First and Second Motifs through Rnd 9: 80 sc.
Rnd 10 (Joining rnd): Ch 1, sc in same st and in next 3 sc,
(ch 3, sc in next 4 sc) 5 times, place marker around last ch-3
made for joining placement, (ch 3, sc in next 4 sc) 7 times,
ch 1, holding Motifs with **wrong** sides together, sc in marked
ch-3 sp on **adjacent Motif**, † ch 1, (sc in next 4 sc on **new
Motif**, ch 1, sc in next ch-3 sp on **adjacent Motif**, ch 1)
twice †, sc in next 4 sc on **new Motif**, (ch 3, sc in next 4 sc)
twice, ch 1, holding Motifs with **wrong** sides together, skip next
2 ch-3 sps from previous joining on **adjacent Motif**, sc in next
ch-3 sp, repeat from † to † once; join with slip st to first sc,
finish off.

25TH
Work same as First and Second Motifs through Rnd 9: 80 sc.
Rnd 10 (Joining rnd): Ch 1, sc in same st and in next 3 sc,
(ch 3, sc in next 4 sc) 17 times, ch 1, holding Motifs with
wrong sides together, skip next 2 ch-3 sps from previous
joining on **adjacent Motif**, sc in next ch-3 sp, ch 1, (sc in next
4 sc on **new Motif**, ch 1, sc in next ch-3 sp on **adjacent Motif**,
ch 1) twice; join with slip st to first sc, finish off.

26TH
Work same as First and Second Motifs.

27TH
Work same as Sixth Motif.

28TH THROUGH 32ND
Work same as Seventh Motif.

Continued on page 74.

33RD

Work same as First and Second Motifs through Rnd 9: 80 sc.
Rnd 10 (Joining rnd)**:** Ch 1, sc in same st and in next 3 sc,
(ch 3, sc in next 4 sc) 5 times, place marker around last ch-3
made for joining placement, (ch 3, sc in next 4 sc) 7 times,
† ch 1, holding Motifs with **wrong** sides together, skip next
2 ch-3 sps from previous joining on **adjacent Motif**, sc in next
ch-3 sp, ch 1, (sc in next 4 sc on **new Motif**, ch 1, sc in next
ch-3 sp on **adjacent Motif**, ch 1) twice †, sc in next 4 sc on
new Motif, (ch 3, sc in next 4 sc) twice, repeat from † to †
once; join with slip st to first sc, finish off.

34TH

Work same as Eighth Motif.

35TH

Work same as First and Second Motifs.

36TH

Work same as First and Second Motifs through Rnd 9: 80 sc.
Rnd 10 (Joining rnd)**:** Ch 1, sc in same st and in next 3 sc,
(ch 3, sc in next 4 sc) 5 times, place marker around last ch-3
made for joining placement, (ch 3, sc in next 4 sc) 7 times,
ch 1, holding Motifs with **wrong** sides together, skip next
2 ch-3 sps from previous joining on **adjacent Motif**, sc in next
ch-3 sp, ch 1, (sc in next 4 sc on **new Motif**, ch 1, sc in next
ch-3 sp on **adjacent Motif**, ch 1) twice, sc in next 4 sc on **new
Motif**, (ch 3, sc in next 4 sc) twice, ch 1, holding Motifs with
wrong sides together, sc in any ch-3 sp on **adjacent Motif**,
ch 1, (sc in next 4 sc on **new Motif**, ch 1, sc in next ch-3 sp on
adjacent Motif, ch 1) twice; join with slip st to first sc,
finish off.

37TH THROUGH 41ST

Work same as Seventh Motif.

42ND

Work same as 33rd Motif.

43RD

Work same as Eighth Motif.

44TH

Work same as First and Second Motifs through Rnd 9: 80 sc.
Rnd 10 (Joining rnd)**:** Ch 1, sc in same st and in next 3 sc,
(ch 3, sc in next 4 sc) 17 times, ch 1, holding Motifs with
wrong sides together, sc in marked ch-3 sp on **adjacent
Motif**, ch 1, (sc in next 4 sc on **new** Motif, ch 1, sc in next
ch-3 sp on **adjacent Motif**, ch 1) twice; join with slip st to first
sc, finish off.

45TH

Work same as 33rd Motif.

46TH THROUGH 48TH

Work same as Seventh Motif.

49TH

Work same as 33rd Motif.

50TH

Work same as Eighth Motif.

51ST

Work same as 44th Motif.

52ND

Work same as 33rd Motif.

53RD

Work same as Seventh Motif.

54TH

Work same as 33rd Motif.

55TH

Work same as Eighth Motif.

56TH

Work same as 44th Motif.

57TH

Work same as 33rd Motif.

58TH

Work same as Eighth Motif.

59TH

Work same as 44th Motif.

FILL-IN MOTIF

With Green, ch 4; join with slip st to form a ring.

Rnd 1: Ch 2, 12 hdc in ring; join with slip st to first hdc: 12 hdc.

Rnd 2: Ch 1, sc in same st, ch 5, sc in next hdc, ★ (ch 3, sc in next hdc) twice, ch 5, sc in next hdc; repeat from ★ 2 times **more**, ch 3, sc in last hdc, ch 3; join with slip st to first sc: 4 ch-5 sps and 8 ch-3 sps.

Rnd 3: Slip st in first ch-5 sp, ch 1, 4 sc in same sp, 2 sc in each of next 2 ch-3 sps, ★ 4 sc in next ch-5 sp, 2 sc in each of next 2 ch-3 sps; repeat from ★ 2 times **more**; join with slip st to first sc: 32 sc.

Rnd 4 (Joining rnd): Work Three or Four Side Joining.

THREE SIDE JOINING

Rnd 4 (Joining rnd): Ch 1, sc in same st and in next 3 sc, (ch 3, sc in next 4 sc) twice, ch 1, with **right** side of Afghan facing and working in sps along edge of Afghan, skip next ch-3 sp on **Motif** to **right** of joining, sc in next ch-3 sp, ch 1, sc in next 4 sc on **Fill-In Motif**, ch 1, sc in next ch-3 sp on **Motif**, ch 1, ★ sc in next 2 sc on **Fill-In Motif**, ch 3, sc in next joining between Motifs, ch 3, sc in next 2 sc on **Fill-In Motif**, ch 1, sc in next ch-3 sp on **Motif**, ch 1, sc in next 4 sc on **Fill-In Motif**, ch 1, sc in next ch-3 sp on **Motif**, ch 1; repeat from ★ once **more**; join with slip st to first sc, finish off.

Repeat in each sp between joined Motifs along outside edges of Afghan.

FOUR SIDE JOINING

Rnd 4 (Joining rnd): Slip st in next sc, ch 1, sc in same st, ch 3, with **right** side of Afghan facing and working in sps between joined Motifs, sc in any joining between Motifs, ch 3, sc in next 2 sc on **Fill-In Motif**, ch 1, sc in next ch-3 sp on **Motif**, ch 1, sc in next 4 sc on **Fill-In Motif**, ch 1, sc in next ch-3 sp on **Motif**, ch 1, ★ sc in next 2 sc on **Fill-In Motif**, ch 3, sc in next joining between Motifs, ch 3, sc in next 2 sc on **Fill-In Motif**, ch 1, sc in next ch-3 sp on **Motif**, ch 1, sc in next 4 sc on **Fill-In Motif**, ch 1, sc in next ch-3 sp on **Motif**, ch 1; repeat from ★ 2 times **more**, sc in last st on **Fill-In Motif**; join with slip st to first sc, finish off.

Repeat in each sp between joined Motifs of Afghan.

EDGING

With **right** side facing and working along long edge of Afghan, join Green with sc in joining between First Motif and Fill-In Motif *(see Joining With Sc, page 142)*; ★ † ch 5, sc in next ch-3 sp, work Picot, sc in next ch-3 sp, ch 5, sc in next joining, ch 5, [sc in next ch-3 sp, (work Picot, sc in next ch-3 sp) 7 times, ch 5, sc in next joining, ch 5, sc in next ch-3 sp, work Picot, sc in next ch-3 sp, ch 5, sc in next joining, ch 5] across to next corner Motif, sc in next ch-3 sp, (work Picot, sc in next ch-3 sp) 12 times, ch 5 †, sc in next joining; repeat from ★ 2 times **more**, then repeat from † to † once; join with slip st to first sc, finish off.

EDGING

Ch 1, turn; sc in first dc, ch 3, dc in next ch, ch 3, skip next dc, (sc in next dc, ch 3) twice, skip next dc, sc in next dc, ch 3, skip next dc, ★ pull up a loop in next dc and in next ch, YO and draw through all 3 loops on hook, ch 3, skip next dc, (sc in next dc, ch 3) twice, skip next dc, sc in next dc, ch 3, skip next dc; repeat from ★ across to last ch-2 sp, skip next ch, dc in next ch, ch 3, sc in last dc, ch 3; working across end of rows, (sc in top of next row, ch 3) across; working in free loops of beginning ch *(Fig. 21b, page 142)*, sc in first ch, ch 3, (skip next 2 chs, sc in next ch, ch 3) 60 times; working across end of rows, (sc in top of next row, ch 3) across; join with slip st to first sc, finish off.

Holding 6 strands of Green together, each 16" long, add fringe in each ch-3 sp across short edges of Afghan *(Figs. 27a & c, page 143)*.

Row 15: Ch 4, turn; (dc in next dc, ch 1) twice, ★ skip next dc, dc in next dc and in next 2 chs, ch 4, skip next sc, sc in next sc, ch 4, skip next sc and next 2 chs, dc in next 2 chs and in next dc, ch 1, skip next dc, (dc in next dc, ch 1) twice; repeat from ★ across to last dc, dc in last dc: 140 dc.

Row 16: Ch 4, turn; (dc in next dc, ch 1) 3 times, skip next dc, dc in next dc and in next 2 chs, ch 1, skip next sc and next 2 chs, dc in next 2 chs and in next dc, ch 1, ★ skip next dc, (dc in next dc, ch 1) 4 times, skip next dc, dc in next dc and in next 2 chs, ch 1, skip next sc and next 2 chs, dc in next 2 chs and in next dc, ch 1; repeat from ★ across to last 5 dc, skip next dc, dc in next dc, (ch 1, dc in next dc) 3 times: 174 dc and 105 ch-1 sps.

Row 17: Ch 4, turn; (dc in next dc, ch 1) 4 times, skip next dc, dc in next dc, dc in next ch-1 sp and in next dc, ch 1, ★ skip next dc, (dc in next dc, ch 1) 6 times, skip next dc, dc in next dc, dc in next ch-1 sp and in next dc, ch 1; repeat from ★ across to last 6 dc, skip next dc, dc in next dc, (ch 1, dc in next dc) 4 times: 157 dc and 122 ch-1 sps.

Row 18: Ch 4, turn; (dc in next dc, ch 1) 5 times, ★ skip next dc, (dc in next dc, ch 1) 8 times; repeat from ★ across to last 7 dc, skip next dc, dc in next dc, (ch 1, dc in next dc) 5 times: 140 dc and 139 ch-1 sps.

Row 19: Ch 3, turn; dc in next ch-1 sp and in each dc and each ch-1 sp across: 279 dc.

Row 20: Ch 4, turn; skip next dc, dc in next dc, ★ ch 1, skip next dc, dc in next dc; repeat from ★ across: 140 dc and 139 ch-1 sps.

Row 21: Ch 3, turn; dc in next ch-1 sp and in next dc, ★ ch 1, dc in next dc, dc in next ch-1 sp and in next dc; repeat from ★ across: 210 dc and 69 ch-1 sps.

Rows 22-105: Repeat Rows 2-21, 4 times; then repeat Rows 2-5 once **more**; do **not** finish off.

EDGING

Rnd 1: Ch 4, do **not** turn; working in end of rows, skip first row, (dc in next row, ch 1) across; working in free loops of beginning ch *(Fig. 21b, page 142)*, (dc, ch 1) twice in first ch, skip next ch, (dc in next ch, ch 1, skip next ch) 138 times, (dc, ch 1) twice in next ch; working in end of rows, skip first row, (dc in next row, ch 1) across; working across dc on Row 105, (dc, ch 1) twice in first dc, ★ skip next dc, (dc in next dc, ch 1) twice; repeat from ★ across to last 2 dc, skip next dc, dc in last dc, ch 1; join with slip st to first dc: 492 dc.

Rnd 2: Ch 3, dc in next ch-1 sp and in each dc and each ch-1 sp around working 3 dc in each corner ch-1 sp; join with slip st to first dc, finish off.

Holding 5 strands of yarn together, each 16" long, add fringe evenly across short edges of Afghan *(Figs. 27a & c, page 143)*.

Rnd 10: With **right** side facing, join Lt Rose with slip st in any corner ch-2 sp; ch 3, (2 dc, ch 2, 3 dc) in same sp, skip next 3 dc, (3 dc in sp **before** next dc, skip next 5 dc, 3 dc in sp **before** next dc, skip next 3 dc) twice, ★ (3 dc, ch 2, 3 dc) in next corner ch-2 sp, skip next 3 dc, (3 dc in sp **before** next dc, skip next 5 dc, 3 dc in sp **before** next dc, skip next 3 dc) twice; repeat from ★ 2 times **more**; join with slip st to first dc, finish off: 72 dc.

Rnd 11: With **right** side facing, join Ecru with slip st in any corner ch-2 sp; ch 3, (2 dc, ch 2, 3 dc) in same sp, skip next 3 dc, 3 dc in sp **before** next dc, skip next 3 dc, (5 dc in sp **before** next dc, skip next 3 dc, 3 dc in sp **before** next dc, skip next 3 dc) twice, ★ (3 dc, ch 2, 3 dc) in next corner ch-2 sp, skip next 3 dc, 3 dc in sp **before** next dc, skip next 3 dc, (5 dc in sp **before** next dc, skip next 3 dc, 3 dc in sp **before** next dc, skip next 3 dc) twice; repeat from ★ 2 times **more**; join with slip st to first dc, finish off: 100 dc.

Rnd 12: With **right** side facing, join Green with slip st in any corner ch-2 sp; ch 3, 4 dc in same sp, ★ † skip next dc, 2 dc in next dc, hdc in next dc, slip st in next dc, skip next 2 dc, hdc in next dc, 2 dc in next dc, 3 dc in next dc, 2 dc in next dc, hdc in next dc, slip st in next dc, skip next 3 dc, hdc in next dc, 2 dc in next dc, 3 dc in next dc, 2 dc in next dc, hdc in next dc, slip st in next dc, skip next 2 dc, hdc in next dc, 2 dc in next dc †, 5 dc in next corner ch-2 sp; repeat from ★ 2 times **more**, then repeat from † to † once; join with slip st to first dc, finish off: 128 sts.

REMAINING 7 SQUARES

Work same as First Square through Rnd 11: 100 dc.

Rnd 12 (Joining rnd): With **right** side facing, join Green with slip st in second dc to left of any corner ch-2 sp; ch 3, dc in same st, ★ † hdc in next dc, slip st in next dc, skip next 2 dc, hdc in next dc, 2 dc in next dc, 3 dc in next dc, 2 dc in next dc, hdc in next dc, slip st in next dc, skip next 3 dc, hdc in next dc, 2 dc in next dc, 3 dc in next dc, 2 dc in next dc, hdc in next dc, slip st in next dc, skip next 2 dc, hdc in next dc, 2 dc in next dc †, 5 dc in next corner ch-2 sp, skip next dc, 2 dc in next dc; repeat from ★ once **more**, then repeat from † to † once, 4 dc in next corner ch-2 sp, join Squares, dc in same sp on **new Square**, join Squares, skip next dc on **new Square**, 2 dc in next dc, hdc in next dc, slip st in next dc, skip next 2 dc, ♥ hdc in next dc, 2 dc in each of next 2 dc, join Squares, dc in same st on **new Square**, join Squares, 2 dc in next dc on **new Square**, hdc in next dc, slip st in next dc ♥, skip next 3 dc, repeat from ♥ to ♥ once, skip next 2 dc, hdc in next dc, 2 dc in next dc, join Squares, dc in corner ch-2 sp on **new Square**, join Squares, 4 dc in same sp on **new Square**; join with slip st to first dc, finish off.

BORDER

Rnd 1: With **right** side facing and working across short edge, join Ecru with slip st in center dc of first corner 5-dc group; ch 3, (dc, ch 1, 2 dc) in same st, † dc in next 4 dc, work Cluster, (dc in same st and in next 6 dc, work Cluster) twice, dc in same st and in next 3 dc †, (2 dc, ch 1, 2 dc) in next dc, repeat from † to † once, (work Joining Cluster, repeat from † to † once) 7 times, [(2 dc, ch 1, 2 dc) in next dc, repeat from † to † once] twice, (work Joining Cluster, repeat from † to † once) 7 times; join with slip st to first dc, finish off: 480 sts and 4 ch-1 sps.

Rnd 2: With **right** side facing, join Rose with slip st in any corner ch-1 sp; ch 2 **(counts as first hdc, now and throughout)**, 2 hdc in same sp, hdc in next dc and in each st around working 3 hdc in each corner ch-1 sp; join with slip st to first hdc, finish off: 492 hdc.

ASSEMBLY

With Rose and working through both loops, whipstitch Panels together **(Fig. 26b, page 143)**, beginning in center hdc of first corner 3-hdc group and ending in center hdc of next corner 3-hdc group.

EDGING

Rnd 1: With **right** side facing, join Rose with slip st in center hdc of top right corner 3-hdc group; ch 2, (hdc, ch 1, 2 hdc) in same st, ★ † hdc in next 31 hdc and in same st as joining, hdc in joining and in same st as joining on next Square; repeat from ★ 3 times **more**, hdc in next 31 hdc, (2 hdc, ch 1, 2 hdc) in next hdc, 2 hdc in next hdc, hdc in next hdc and in each hdc across to next corner 3-hdc group, 2 hdc in next hdc †, (2 hdc, ch 1, 2 hdc) in next hdc, repeat from † to † once; join with slip st to first hdc: 780 hdc and 4 ch-1 sps.

Rnd 2: Hdc in next hdc, (3 dc, ch 2, 3 dc) in next corner ch-1 sp, hdc in next hdc, ★ (slip st in next hdc, hdc in next hdc, dc in next hdc, 3 tr in next hdc, dc in next hdc, hdc in next hdc) across to within 2 hdc of next corner ch-1 sp, slip st in next hdc, hdc in next hdc, (3 dc, ch 2, 3 dc) in next corner ch-1 sp, hdc in next hdc; repeat from ★ 2 times **more**, (slip st in next hdc, hdc in next hdc, dc in next hdc, 3 tr in next hdc, dc in next hdc, hdc in next hdc) across; join with slip st to first st, finish off.

SEASIDE DREAMS

*As beautiful as the treasures of the sea, our airy afghan
is ideal for a breezy summer evening. Soft pastel yarns and rows
of shells reflect images of the shore in a bedroom or den.*

Finished Size: 46" x 69"

MATERIALS
  Worsted Weight Yarn:
    Peach - 23 ounces,
      (650 grams, 1,575 yards)
    Ecru - 21 ounces,
      (600 grams, 1,440 yards)
  Crochet hook, size H (5.00 mm) **or** size
    needed for gauge

GAUGE SWATCH: 7"w x 5"h
With Peach, ch 26 **loosely**.
Work same as Afghan Body for 12 rows.

AFGHAN BODY
With Peach, ch 161 **loosely**.
Row 1 (Wrong side)**:** Sc in second ch from hook, ★ ch 3, skip next 2 chs, sc in next ch; repeat from ★ across; finish off: 53 ch-3 sps.
Note: Loop a short piece of yarn around the **back** of any stitch to mark **right** side.
Row 2: With **right** side facing, join Ecru with slip st in first sc; ch 4 **(counts as first dc plus ch 1, now and throughout)**, sc in next ch-3 sp, ch 1, 5 dc in next ch-3 sp, ch 1, sc in next ch-3 sp, ★ (ch 3, sc in next ch-3 sp) 3 times, ch 1, 5 dc in next ch-3 sp, ch 1, sc in next ch-3 sp; repeat from ★ across, ch 1, dc in last sc; finish off: 11 5-dc groups and 30 ch-3 sps.
Row 3: With **wrong** side facing, join Peach with sc in first dc *(see Joining With Sc, page 142)*; ch 3, (skip next dc, sc in next dc, ch 3) twice, ★ skip next ch-1 sp, sc in next ch-3 sp, ch 1, 5 dc in next ch-3 sp, ch 1, sc in next ch-3 sp, ch 3, (skip next dc, sc in next dc, ch 3) twice; repeat from ★ across to last 2 dc, skip next dc, sc in last dc; finish off: 10 5-dc groups and 33 ch-3 sps.
Row 4: With **right** side facing, join Ecru with slip st in first sc; ch 4, sc in next ch-3 sp, ch 1, 5 dc in next ch-3 sp, ch 1, sc in next ch-3 sp, ★ ch 3, (skip next dc, sc in next dc, ch 3) twice, skip next ch-1 sp, sc in next ch-3 sp, ch 1, 5 dc in next ch-3 sp, ch 1, sc in next ch-3 sp; repeat from ★ across to last sc, ch 1, dc in last sc; finish off: 11 5-dc groups and 30 ch-3 sps.
Repeat Rows 3 and 4 until Afghan Body measures approximately 66¹/₂ " from beginning ch, ending by working Row 4.
Last Row: With **wrong** side facing, join Peach with slip st in first dc; ch 5 **(counts as first dc plus ch 2)**, (skip next dc, sc in next dc, ch 2) twice, ★ skip next ch-1 sp, dc in next ch-3 sp, ch 2, sc in next ch-3 sp, ch 2, dc in next ch-3 sp, ch 2, (skip next dc, sc in next dc, ch 2) twice; repeat from ★ across to last 2 dc, skip next dc, dc in last dc; do **not** finish off: 54 sts and 53 ch-2 sps.

EDGING

Rnd 1: Ch 1, turn; sc in first dc and in each ch and each st across to last dc, (sc, ch 2, sc) in last dc; work 232 sc evenly spaced across end of rows, ch 2; working in free loops of beginning ch *(Fig. 21b, page 142)*, sc in ch at base of first sc and in each ch across, ch 2; work 232 sc evenly spaced across end of rows, sc in same st as first sc, ch 2; join with slip st to first sc: 786 sc and 4 ch-2 sps.

Rnd 2: Ch 3, do **not** turn; ★ dc in next sc and in each sc across to next corner ch-2 sp, dc in corner ch-2 sp, (ch 1, dc in same sp) twice; repeat from ★ around; join with slip st to top of beginning ch-3: 798 sts and 8 ch-1 sps.

Rnd 3: Ch 1, sc in same st, ★ sc in each dc across to next ch-1 sp, sc in ch-1 sp, (sc, ch 1, sc) in next dc, sc in next ch-1 sp; repeat from ★ around to last dc, sc in last dc; join with slip st to first sc, finish off.

79

QUIET COMFORT

Whispers of blue and gold bring quiet comfort to a delicately stitched throw. A scalloped edging and flowing fringe add sophistication to the intricate afghan.

Finished Size: 48" x 67¹/₂"

MATERIALS
Worsted Weight Yarn:
    Ecru - 40 ounces, (1,140 grams, 2,745 yards)
    Blue - 8 ounces, (230 grams, 550 yards)
    Gold - 6 ounces, (170 grams, 410 yards)
    Crochet hook, size H (5.00 mm) **or** size needed
      for gauge

GAUGE: 5 Shells and 9 rows = 6"

Gauge Swatch: 6" square
With Ecru, ch 24 **loosely**.
Work same as Afghan Body for 9 rows.

Each row is worked across length of Afghan.

STITCH GUIDE

> **SHELL**
> (3 Dc, ch 1, dc) in st or sp indicated.
> **CLUSTER**
> Ch 3, YO, insert hook in third ch from hook, YO and pull up a loop, YO and draw through 2 loops on hook, YO, insert hook in same ch, YO and pull up a loop, YO and draw through 2 loops on hook, YO and draw through all 3 loops on hook *(Figs. 15a & b, page 141)*.

COLOR SEQUENCE
One row **each**: Ecru *(Fig. 22a, page 142)*, Blue, Ecru, Gold, Ecru, Blue, ★ 3 rows Ecru, one row **each**: Blue, Ecru, Gold, Ecru, Blue; repeat from ★ throughout, 1 row Ecru.

AFGHAN BODY

With Ecru, ch 228 **loosely**.
Row 1 (Right side)**:** Work Shell in fourth ch from hook **(3 skipped chs count as first dc)**, (skip next 3 chs, work Shell in next ch) across to last 4 chs, skip next 3 chs, dc in last ch changing to next color: 56 Shells.
Note: Loop a short piece of yarn around any stitch to mark Row 1 as **right** side.
Row 2: Ch 3 **(counts as first dc, now and throughout)**, turn; (dc, work Cluster, ch 2, dc) in each ch-1 sp across, skip next 3 dc, dc in last dc: 56 Clusters.
Row 3: Ch 3, turn; keeping Clusters to **right** side of work, work Shell in each ch-2 sp across, skip next dc, dc in last dc: 56 Shells.
Rows 4-71: Repeat Rows 2 and 3, 34 times.
Finish off.

EDGING
FIRST SIDE
With **right** side facing, join Ecru with slip st in first dc; ch 3, tr in same st, (slip st, ch 3, tr) in each ch-1 sp across to last ch-1 sp, (slip st, ch 2, dc) in last ch-1 sp, skip next dc, slip st in last dc; finish off.

SECOND SIDE
With **right** side facing and working in sps and free loops of beginning ch *(Fig. 21b, page 142)*, join Ecru with slip st in first ch; ch 2, dc in same ch, (slip st, ch 3, tr) in each sp across, skip next ch, slip st in next ch; finish off.

Holding 6 strands of Ecru together, each 18" long, add fringe evenly across short edges of Afghan *(Figs. 27b & d, page 143)*.

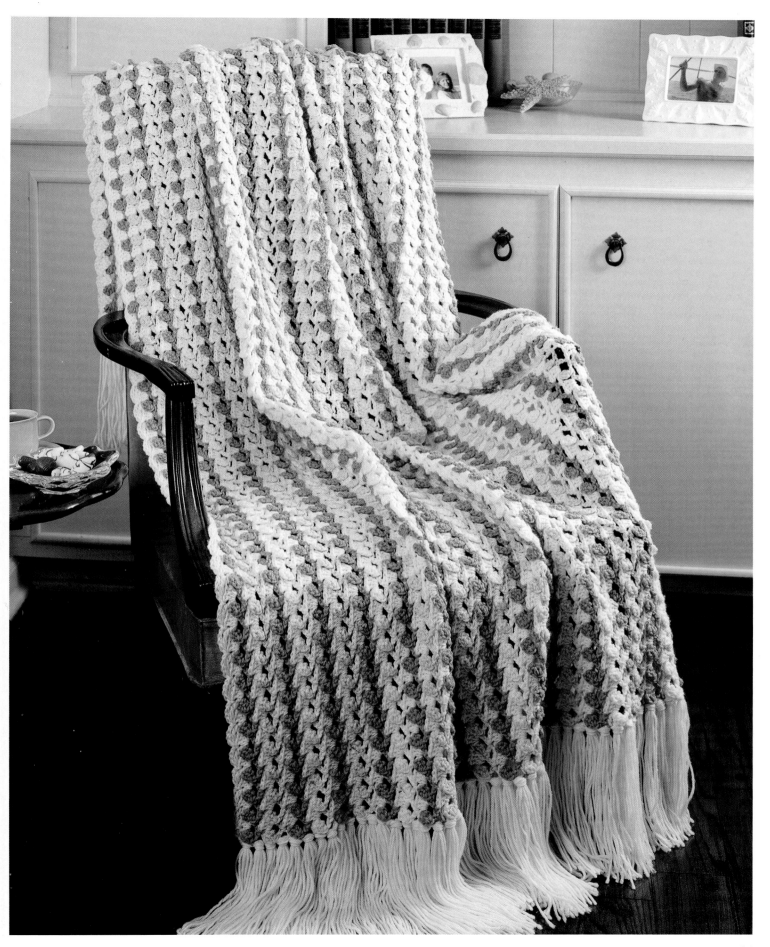

PATRIOTIC SALUTE

Salute Independence Day with our bold afghan. The all-American throw features star-spangled squares that are whipstitched together and finished with a tailored edging.

Finished Size: 56" x 67"

MATERIALS
Worsted Weight Yarn:
  Red - 32 ounces, (910 grams, 1,810 yards)
  White - 16 ounces, (450 grams, 905 yards)
  Blue - 16 ounces, (450 grams, 905 yards)
Crochet hook, size J (6.00 mm) **or** size needed
  for gauge
Yarn needle

GAUGE: Each Square = 7¾"

STITCH GUIDE

PUFF ST
★ YO, insert hook in sp indicated, YO and pull up a loop even with loop on hook; repeat from ★ 2 times **more**, YO and draw through all 7 loops on hook.

DECREASE
YO, insert hook in same st as joining on **same** Square, YO and pull up a loop, YO, insert hook in same st as joining on **next** Square, YO and pull up a loop, YO and draw through all 5 loops on hook.

SQUARE (Make 50)
With White, ch 6; join with slip st to form a ring.
Rnd 1 (Right side): Pull up a 1¼" loop, (work Puff St in ring, ch 5) 5 times; join with slip st to top of first Puff St, finish off: 5 ch-5 sps.
Note: Loop a short piece of yarn around any stitch to mark Rnd 1 as **right** side.
Rnd 2: With **right** side facing, join Blue with sc in any ch-5 sp **(see Joining With Sc, page 142)**; 5 sc in same sp, 6 sc in each ch-5 sp around; join with slip st to first sc: 30 sc.
Rnd 3: Ch 1, sc in same st and in next 3 sc, 2 sc in next sc, (sc in next 4 sc, 2 sc in next sc) around; join with slip st to first sc: 36 sc.
Rnd 4: Ch 1, sc in same st and in next 3 sc, hdc in next sc, dc in next sc, 3 tr in next sc, dc in next sc, hdc in next sc, ★ sc in next 4 sc, hdc in next sc, dc in next sc, 3 tr in next sc, dc in next sc, hdc in next sc; repeat from ★ 2 times **more**; join with slip st to first sc, finish off: 44 sts.

Rnd 5: With **right** side facing and working in Back Loops Only **(Fig. 20, page 142)**, join Red with slip st in any st; ch 3 **(counts as first dc, now and throughout)**, dc in each st around working 5 dc in center tr of each corner 3-tr group; join with slip st to first dc, finish off: 60 dc.
Rnd 6: With **right** side facing and working in Back Loops Only, join White with slip st in any dc; ch 3, dc in each dc around working 5 dc in center dc of each corner 5-dc group; join with slip st to first dc, finish off: 76 dc.
Rnd 7: With **right** side facing and working in Back Loops Only, join Red with slip st in any dc; ch 2 **(counts as first hdc, now and throughout)**, hdc in each dc around working 5 hdc in center dc of each corner 5-dc group; join with slip st to first hdc, finish off: 92 hdc.

ASSEMBLY
With Red, using Placement Diagram as a guide, and working through inside loops only, whipstitch Squares together **(Fig. 26a, page 143)**, beginning in center hdc of first corner 5-hdc group and ending in center hdc of next corner 5-hdc group.

PLACEMENT DIAGRAM

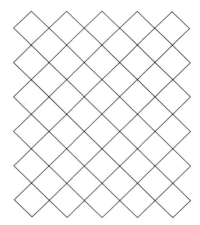

EDGING
With **right** side facing and working in both loops, join Red with slip st in any hdc; ch 2 **(counts as first hdc)**, hdc in each hdc around working 3 hdc in center hdc of each corner 5-hdc group and decrease at each joining; join with slip st to first hdc, finish off.

SEASHELL ILLUSION

A lattice-like design creates the illusion of shell motifs on our openweave throw. Relaxing to crochet, this pattern will become a favorite you'll want to make again and again.

Finished Size: 48" x 60"

MATERIALS
Worsted Weight Yarn:
45½ ounces, (1,290 grams, 2,575 yards)
Crochet hook, size H (5.00 mm) **or** size needed
for gauge

GAUGE: In pattern, 2 repeats = 4½"

STITCH GUIDE

DECREASE (uses next 5 dc)
YO, insert hook in next dc, YO and pull up a loop, YO and draw through 2 loops on hook, YO, skip next 3 dc, insert hook in next dc, YO and pull up a loop, YO and draw through 2 loops on hook, YO and draw through all 3 loops on hook **(counts as one dc)**.

ENDING DECREASE (uses last 3 dc)
YO, insert hook in next dc, YO and pull up a loop, YO and draw through 2 loops on hook, YO, skip next dc, insert hook in last dc, YO and pull up a loop, YO and draw through 2 loops on hook, YO and draw through all 3 loops on hook **(counts as one dc)**.

CLUSTER
YO, insert hook in **same** sc just worked into, YO and pull up a loop, YO and draw through 2 loops on hook, YO, skip next 2 sc, insert hook in **next** sc, YO and pull up a loop, YO and draw through 2 loops on hook, YO and draw through all 3 loops on hook *(Figs. 16a & b, page 141)*.

AFGHAN BODY

Ch 203 **loosely**, place marker in third ch from hook for st placement.

Row 1 (Right side)**:** Working in back ridges of beginning ch *(Fig. 2b, page 139)*, dc in fourth ch from hook **(3 skipped chs count as first dc)** and in next ch, skip next 2 chs, (dc, ch 3, dc) in next ch, ★ skip next 2 chs, dc in next 5 chs, skip next 2 chs, (dc, ch 3, dc) in next ch; repeat from ★ across to last 5 chs, skip next 2 chs, dc in last 3 chs: 141 dc and 20 ch-3 sps.

Note: Loop a short piece of yarn around any stitch to mark Row 1 as **right** side.

Row 2: Ch 3 **(counts as first dc, now and throughout)**, turn; skip next dc, dc in next dc, ch 2, 5 dc in next ch-3 sp, ch 2, ★ skip next dc, decrease, ch 2, 5 dc in next ch-3 sp, ch 2; repeat from ★ across to last 4 dc, skip next dc, work ending decrease: 122 dc and 40 ch-2 sps.

Row 3: Ch 4 **(counts as first dc plus ch 1)**, turn; dc in same st and in next 5 dc, ★ (dc, ch 3, dc) in next dc, dc in next 5 dc; repeat from ★ across to last 2 dc, (dc, ch 1, dc) in next dc, leave remaining dc unworked: 142 dc and 21 sps.

Row 4: Ch 3, turn; 2 dc in next ch-1 sp, ch 2, skip next dc, decrease, ch 2, ★ 5 dc in next ch-3 sp, ch 2, skip next dc, decrease, ch 2; repeat from ★ across to last ch-1 sp, 2 dc in ch-1 sp, dc in last dc: 121 dc and 40 ch-2 sps.

Row 5: Ch 3, turn; dc in next 2 dc, (dc, ch 3, dc) in next dc, ★ dc in next 5 dc, (dc, ch 3, dc) in next dc; repeat from ★ across to last 3 dc, dc in last 3 dc: 141 dc and 20 ch-3 sps.
Repeat Rows 2-5 until Afghan Body measures approximately 58" from beginning ch, ending by working a **wrong** side row; do **not** finish off.

EDGING

Rnd 1: Ch 1, turn; 2 sc in first dc, work 165 sc evenly spaced across to last dc, 3 sc in last dc; work 216 sc evenly spaced across end of rows; working in free loops of beginning ch *(Fig. 21b, page 142)*, 3 sc in first ch, work 165 sc evenly spaced across to marked ch, 3 sc in marked ch; work 216 sc evenly spaced across end of rows, sc in same st as first sc; join with slip st to first sc: 774 sc.

Rnd 2: Ch 6 **(counts as first dc plus ch 3)**, dc in same st, ch 3, (work Cluster, ch 3) across to third sc of next corner 3-sc group, ★ (dc in same center sc, ch 3) twice, (work Cluster, ch 3) across to third sc of next corner 3-sc group; repeat from ★ around working last Cluster in same st as first dc; join with slip st to first dc: 266 ch-3 sps.

Rnd 3: Slip st in first ch-3 sp, ch 1, sc in same sp, (ch 3, sc in same sp) twice, ★ (sc, ch 3, sc) in each ch-3 sp across to next corner ch-3 sp, sc in corner ch-3 sp, (ch 3, sc in same sp) twice; repeat from ★ 2 times **more**, (sc, ch 3, sc) in each ch-3 sp across; join with slip st to first sc, finish off.

WINDOWPANE WRAP

august

Panes of color turn this plush wrap into a one-of-a-kind throw. Its checkered effect is achieved by working treble crochet stitches over a previously worked row. When the afghan is reversed, the design turns into a medley of stripes.

Finished Size: 46¹/₂ " x 62"

MATERIALS
Worsted Weight Yarn:
 Off-White - 31¹/₂ ounces,
  (890 grams, 1,780 yards)
 Blue - 7 ounces,
  (200 grams, 395 yards)
 Yellow - 7 ounces,
  (200 grams, 395 yards)
 Lt Green - 7 ounces,
  (200 grams, 395 yards)
 Green - 7 ounces,
  (200 grams, 395 yards)
 Pink - 7 ounces,
  (200 grams, 395 yards)
 Lavender - 7 ounces,
  (200 grams, 395 yards)
 Red - 7 ounces,
  (200 grams, 395 yards)
Crochet hook, size H (5.00 mm) **or** size
 needed for gauge

GAUGE: In pattern, 17 sts and
   13 rows = 5"

Gauge Swatch: 5¹/₂ "w x 5"h
With Off-White, ch 20 **loosely**.
Work same as Afghan for 13 rows.

Each row is worked across length of Wrap. When joining yarn and finishing off, always leave a 9" end to be worked into fringe.

COLOR SEQUENCE
One row **each**: Off-White, Blue, Off-White, Yellow, Off-White, Green, Off-White, Pink, Off-White, ★ Lavender, Off-White, Red, Off-White, Lt Green, Off-White, Blue, Off-White, Yellow, Off-White, Green, Off-White, Pink, Off-White; repeat from ★ throughout.

AFGHAN
With Off-White, ch 212 **loosely**.
Row 1 (Wrong side)**:** Sc in back ridge of second ch from hook *(Fig. 2b, page 139)* and each ch across; finish off: 211 sc.
Note: Loop a short piece of yarn around **back** of any stitch to mark **right** side.
Row 2: With **right** side facing, join next color with slip st in first sc; ch 3 **(counts as first dc, now and throughout)**, dc in next 2 sc, ch 1, ★ skip next sc, dc in next 2 sc, ch 1; repeat from ★ across to last 4 sc, skip next sc, dc in last 3 sc; finish off: 142 dc and 69 ch-1 sps.
Row 3: With **wrong** side facing, join Off-White with sc in first dc *(see Joining With Sc, page 142)*; ★ sc in next 2 dc, working **behind** next ch-1, tr in sc one row **below** ch-1; repeat from ★ across to last 3 dc, sc in last 3 dc; finish off: 211 sts.
Row 4: With **right** side facing, join next color with slip st in first sc; ch 3, dc in next 2 sc, ch 1, ★ skip next tr, dc in next 2 sc, ch 1; repeat from ★ across to last 4 sts, skip next tr, dc in last 3 sc; finish off: 142 dc and 69 ch-1 sps.
Row 5: With **wrong** side facing, join Off-White with sc in first dc; ★ sc in next 2 dc, working **behind** next ch-1, tr in tr one row **below** ch-1; repeat from ★ across to last 3 dc, sc in last 3 dc; finish off: 211 sts.
Rows 6-121: Repeat Rows 4 and 5, 58 times.

Holding 3 strands **each** of Off-White and corresponding color together, each 18" long, add additional fringe across short edges of Wrap *(Figs. 27b & d, page 143)*.

PEBBLE BEACH

Cluster stitches create a sprinkling of "pebbles" across this inviting shell afghan. The lacy openweave pattern makes our rosy throw perfect for quiet summertime nights.

Finished Size: 47" x 64"

MATERIALS
Worsted Weight Yarn:
38¹/₂ ounces, (1,090 grams, 2,640 yards)
Crochet hook, size H (5.00 mm) **or** size needed
for gauge

GAUGE SWATCH: 9"w x 4"h
Ch 36 **loosely.**
Work same as Afghan Body for 6 rows.
Finish off.

STITCH GUIDE

SHELL
(2 Dc, ch 2, 2 dc) in ch-2 sp indicated.
CLUSTER
Ch 3, YO, insert hook in third ch from hook, YO and pull up
a loop, YO and draw through 2 loops on hook, ★ YO, insert
hook in **same** ch, YO and pull up a loop, YO and draw
through 2 loops on hook; repeat from ★ once **more**, YO
and draw through all 4 loops on hook *(Figs. 15a & b,
page 141)*.

AFGHAN BODY

Ch 176 **loosely**, place marker in fourth ch from hook for
st placement.

Row 1: Dc in sixth ch from hook, ★ ch 1, skip next ch, dc in
next ch; repeat from ★ across: 87 sts and 86 ch-1 sps.

Row 2 (Right side): Ch 3 **(counts as first dc, now and
throughout)**, turn; 2 dc in next dc, ch 2, 2 dc in next ch, ch 1,
skip next dc, dc in next dc, ch 1, skip next ch, 2 dc in next ch,
ch 2, 2 dc in next dc, ★ ch 2, skip next dc, dc in next dc and in
next ch, ch 4, dc in next ch and in next dc, ch 2, skip next dc,
2 dc in next dc, ch 2, 2 dc in next ch, ch 1, skip next dc, dc in
next dc, ch 1, skip next ch, 2 dc in next ch, ch 2, 2 dc in next
dc; repeat from ★ across to last sp, skip next ch, dc in next ch:
115 dc and 60 sps.

Row 3: Ch 3, turn; work Shell in next ch-2 sp, ch 1, skip next
ch-1 sp, dc in next dc, ch 1, skip next ch-1 sp, work Shell in
next ch-2 sp, ★ skip next ch-2 sp and next dc, tr in next dc,
work Cluster, (dc, work Cluster) twice in next ch-4 sp, tr in next
dc, skip next ch-2 sp, work Shell in next ch-2 sp, ch 1, skip next
ch-1 sp, dc in next dc, ch 1, skip next ch-1 sp, work Shell in
next ch-2 sp; repeat from ★ across to last 3 dc, skip next 2 dc,
dc in last dc: 18 Shells and 24 Clusters.

Row 4: Ch 3, turn; work Shell in next ch-2 sp, ch 1, skip next
ch-1 sp, dc in next dc, ch 1, skip next ch-1 sp, work Shell in
next ch-2 sp, ★ ch 3, skip next Cluster, sc in next dc, ch 5, skip
next Cluster, sc in next dc, ch 3, skip next Cluster, work Shell in
next ch-2 sp, ch 1, skip next ch-1 sp, dc in next dc, ch 1, skip
next ch-1 sp, work Shell in next ch-2 sp; repeat from ★ across
to last 3 dc, skip next 2 dc, dc in last dc: 18 Shells.

Row 5: Ch 3, turn; work Shell in next ch-2 sp, ch 1, skip next
ch-1 sp, dc in next dc, ch 1, skip next ch-1 sp, work Shell in
next ch-2 sp, ★ skip next ch-3 sp, tr in next sc, work Cluster,
(dc, work Cluster) twice in next ch-5 sp, tr in next sc, skip next
ch-3 sp, work Shell in next ch-2 sp, ch 1, skip next ch-1 sp, dc
in next dc, ch 1, skip next ch-1 sp, work Shell in next ch-2 sp;
repeat from ★ across to last 3 dc, skip next 2 dc, dc in last dc.
Repeat Rows 4 and 5 until Afghan Body measures approximately
62¹/₂ " from beginning ch, ending by working Row 4.

Last Row: Ch 5 **(counts as first dc plus ch 2)**, turn; hdc in
next ch-2 sp, ch 1, (tr in next ch-1 sp, ch 1) twice, ★ 2 hdc in
next ch-2 sp, ch 1, tr in next ch-3 sp, ch 1, tr in next sc, ch 1,
hdc in next ch-5 sp, ch 1, tr in next sc, ch 1, tr in next ch-3 sp,
ch 1, 2 hdc in next ch-2 sp, ch 1, (tr in next ch-1 sp, ch 1)
twice; repeat from ★ across to last 5 dc, hdc in next ch-2 sp,
ch 2, skip next 2 dc, dc in last dc; do **not** finish off.

Continued on page 95.

EBB AND FLOW

Like the gentle waves of the ocean, this appealing afghan will calm the spirit with its delicate rows of shells. Cluster stitches add dimension and texture to our pretty wrap.

Finished Size: 45" x 60"

MATERIALS

Worsted Weight Yarn:
> Blue - 17 ounces, (480 grams, 1,165 yards)
> Gold - 14 ounces, (400 grams, 960 yards)
> Ecru - 12 ounces, (340 grams, 825 yards)
> Crochet hook, size H (5.00 mm) **or** size needed for gauge

GAUGE SWATCH: 4"w x 3¹/₂"h
With Blue, ch 18 **loosely**.
Work same as Afghan Body for 9 rows.
Finish off.

STITCH GUIDE

CLUSTER
Ch 3, YO, insert hook in third ch from hook, YO and pull up a loop, YO and draw through 2 loops on hook, YO, insert hook in same ch, YO and pull up a loop, YO and draw through 2 loops on hook, YO and draw through all 3 loops on hook *(Figs. 15a & b, page 141)*.

AFGHAN BODY

With Blue, ch 178 **loosely**.

Row 1: Sc in second ch from hook and in next ch, ch 1, ★ skip next ch, sc in next ch, ch 1; repeat from ★ across to last 3 chs, skip next ch, sc in last 2 chs: 90 sc and 87 ch-1 sps.

Row 2 (Right side)**:** Ch 1, turn; sc in first sc, ch 1, skip next ch-1 sp, (tr, ch 1) 4 times in next ch-1 sp, ★ skip next ch-1 sp, sc in next ch-1 sp, ch 1, skip next ch-1 sp, (tr, ch 1) 4 times in next ch-1 sp; repeat from ★ across to last 3 sc, skip next 2 sc, sc in last sc; finish off: 22 4-tr groups.

Note: Loop a short piece of yarn around any stitch to mark Row 2 as **right** side.

Row 3: With **wrong** side facing, join Ecru with sc in first sc *(see Joining With Sc, page 142)*; ★ (ch 1, sc in next tr) twice, work Cluster, (sc in next tr, ch 1) twice, sc in next sc; repeat from ★ across; finish off: 22 Clusters.

Row 4: With **right** side facing, join Gold with slip st in first sc; ch 4 **(counts as first tr, now and throughout)**, ★ dc in next sc, ch 1, sc in next sc, ch 1, keeping Cluster to **front**, sc in next sc, ch 1, dc in next sc, tr in next sc; repeat from ★ across: 111 sts and 66 ch-1 sps.

Row 5: Ch 1, turn; sc in first tr and in next dc, ch 1, (sc in next sc, ch 1) twice, ★ sc in next dc, ch 1, skip next tr, sc in next dc, ch 1, skip next ch-1 sp, (sc in next sc, ch 1) twice; repeat from ★ across to last ch-1 sp, skip ch-1 sp, sc in last 2 sts: 90 sc and 87 ch-1 sps.

Row 6: Ch 1, turn; sc in first sc, ch 1, skip next ch-1 sp, (tr, ch 1) 4 times in next ch-1 sp, ★ skip next ch-1 sp, sc in next ch-1 sp, ch 1, skip next ch-1 sp, (tr, ch 1) 4 times in next ch-1 sp; repeat from ★ across to last 3 sc, skip next 2 sc, sc in last sc; finish off: 22 4-tr groups.

Row 7: With **wrong** side facing, join Ecru with sc in first sc; ★ (ch 1, sc in next tr) twice, work Cluster, (sc in next tr, ch 1) twice, sc in next sc; repeat from ★ across; finish off: 22 Clusters.

Row 8: With **right** side facing, join Blue with slip st in first sc; ch 4, ★ dc in next sc, ch 1, sc in next sc, ch 1, keeping Cluster to **front**, sc in next sc, ch 1, dc in next sc, tr in next sc; repeat from ★ across: 111 sts and 66 ch-1 sps.

Row 9: Ch 1, turn; sc in first tr and in next dc, ch 1, (sc in next sc, ch 1) twice, ★ sc in next dc, ch 1, skip next tr, sc in next dc, ch 1, skip next ch-1 sp, (sc in next sc, ch 1) twice; repeat from ★ across to last ch-1 sp, skip ch-1 sp, sc in last 2 sts: 90 sc and 87 ch-1 sps.

Row 10: Ch 1, turn; sc in first sc, ch 1, skip next ch-1 sp, (tr, ch 1) 4 times in next ch-1 sp, ★ skip next ch-1 sp, sc in next ch-1 sp, ch 1, skip next ch-1 sp, (tr, ch 1) 4 times in next ch-1 sp; repeat from ★ across to last 3 sc, skip next 2 sc, sc in last sc; finish off: 22 4-tr groups.

Rows 11-153: Repeat Rows 3-10, 17 times; then repeat Rows 3-9 once **more**; at the end of Row 153, do **not** finish off.

Continued on page 95.

BRILLIANT CONTRAST

Bold hues strike a brilliant contrast against an ebony background on this throw. It's perfect for any room! Use scrap yarn to stitch the flower motifs in layers of assorted colors.

Finished Size: 52" x 69"

MATERIALS
Worsted Weight Yarn:
  Black - 36 ounces, (1,020 grams, 2,035 yards)
  Scraps - 26 ounces, (740 grams, 1,470 yards) **total**
    Note: We used 15 different colors.
      Rnds 1-5 of each Motif requires 29 yards.
Crochet hook, size G (4.00 mm) **or** size needed
  for gauge
Yarn needle

GAUGE: Each Motif = 9½ " (from point to point)

Gauge Swatch: 4" diameter
Work same as Motif through Rnd 3.

STITCH GUIDE

SC DECREASE
Pull up a loop in next 2 sc, YO and draw through all 3 loops on hook.
DC DECREASE (uses next 2 sc)
★ YO, insert hook in **next** sc, YO and pull up a loop, YO and draw through 2 loops on hook; repeat from ★ once **more**, YO and draw through all 3 loops on hook.

MOTIF (Make 50)
With Scrap color desired, ch 4; join with slip st to form a ring.
Rnd 1 (Right side): Ch 3 **(counts as first dc, now and throughout)**, 2 dc in ring, ch 1, (3 dc in ring, ch 1) 5 times; join with slip st to first dc, finish off: 18 dc and 6 ch-1 sps.
Note: Loop a short piece of yarn around any stitch to mark Rnd 1 as **right** side.
Rnd 2: With **right** side facing, join Scrap color desired with slip st in any ch-1 sp; ch 3, (dc, ch 1, 2 dc) in same sp, skip next dc, sc in next dc, skip next dc, ★ (2 dc, ch 1, 2 dc) in next ch-1 sp, skip next dc, sc in next dc, skip next dc; repeat from ★ around; join with slip st to first dc, finish off: 30 sts and 6 ch-1 sps.

Rnd 3: With **right** side facing, join Scrap color desired with slip st in any ch-1 sp; ch 3, 6 dc in same sp, skip next 2 dc, sc in next sc, skip next 2 dc, ★ 7 dc in next ch-1 sp, skip next 2 dc, sc in next sc, skip next 2 dc; repeat from ★ around; join with slip st to first dc, finish off: 48 sts.
Rnd 4: With **right** side facing and working in Back Loops Only **(Fig. 20, page 142)**, join Scrap color desired with sc in any sc **(see Joining With Sc, page 142)**; sc in next dc, hdc in next dc, 2 dc in next dc, 3 tr in next dc, 2 dc in next dc, hdc in next dc, ★ sc in next 3 sts, hdc in next dc, 2 dc in next dc, 3 tr in next dc, 2 dc in next dc, hdc in next dc; repeat from ★ around to last dc, sc in last dc; join with slip st to first sc, finish off: 72 sts.
Rnd 5: With **right** side facing and working in Back Loops Only, join Scrap color desired with sc in same st as joining; skip next sc, sc in next hdc, 2 dc in each of next 7 sts, sc in next hdc, ★ (skip next sc, sc in next st) twice, 2 dc in each of next 7 sts, sc in next hdc; repeat from ★ around to last sc, skip last sc; join with slip st to first sc, finish off: 102 sts.
Rnd 6: With **right** side facing and working in Back Loops Only, join Black with sc in seventh dc to left of joining; sc in next dc, 2 sc in next dc, ★ † sc in next 5 dc, skip next 3 sc, sc in next 5 dc, 2 sc in next dc †, sc in next 2 dc, 2 sc in next dc; repeat from ★ 4 times **more**, then repeat from † to † once; join with slip st to **both** loops of first sc, do **not** finish off: 96 sc.
Rnd 7: Working in both loops, slip st in next sc, ch 3, hdc in same st, ★ † hdc in next sc, sc in next 2 sc, sc decrease, hdc in next sc, dc decrease, hdc in next sc, sc decrease, sc in next 2 sc, hdc in next sc, (hdc, dc) in next sc †, ch 2, (dc, hdc) in next sc; repeat from ★ 4 times **more**, then repeat from † to † once, hdc in first dc to form last ch-2 sp: 90 sts and 6 ch-2 sps.
Rnd 8: Ch 1, (sc, ch 2, sc) in same sp, ★ † sc in next 2 sts, hdc in next 3 sts, dc in next 5 sts, hdc in next 3 sts, sc in next 2 sts †, (sc, ch 2, sc) in next ch-2 sp; repeat from ★ 4 times **more**, then repeat from † to † once; join with slip st to first sc, finish off: 102 sts and 6 ch-2 sps.

Continued on page 94.

BRILLIANT CONTRAST Continued from page 92.

HALF MOTIF (Make 8)

With Black, ch 19 **loosely**.

Row 1 (Right side): 2 Dc in fourth ch from hook **(3 skipped chs count as first dc)**, dc in next ch and in each ch across to last ch, 2 dc in last ch: 19 dc.

Note: Mark Row 1 as **right** side.

Rows 2-7: Ch 3, turn; dc in same st and in each dc across to last dc, 2 dc in last dc: 31 dc.

Trim: Ch 2, do **not** turn; † working in end of rows, sc in first row, (3 sc in next row, 2 sc in next row) 3 times †; working in free loops of beginning ch **(Fig. 21b, page 142)**, (sc, ch 2, sc) in first ch, sc in next 15 chs, (sc, ch 2, sc) in next ch, repeat from † to † once, ch 2; join with slip st to top of first dc on Row 7, finish off: 51 sc.

ASSEMBLY

With Black, using Placement Diagram as a guide, and working though both loops, whipstitch Motifs together **(Fig. 26b, page 143)**, forming 5 horizontal strips of 6 Motifs **and** 4 horizontal strips of 5 Motifs and 2 Half Motifs, beginning in second ch of first ch-2 and ending in first ch of next ch-2; whipstitch strips together in same manner.

PLACEMENT DIAGRAM

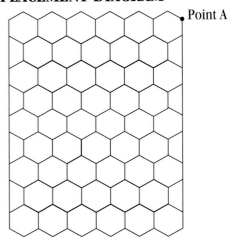

Point A

EDGING

With **right** side facing and working in Back Loops Only, join Black with sc in first ch of ch-2 at Point A; † ch 1, sc in next ch and in each st across to next ch-2, ★ sc in next ch, ch 1, sc in next ch, sc in next 17 sts and in next ch, skip next joining, sc in next ch and in each st across to next ch-2; repeat from ★ 4 times **more**, (sc in next ch, ch 1, sc in next ch and in next 17 sts) twice, (sc in next ch, skip next joining, sc in next ch, sc in next 31 sts and in next ch, skip next joining, sc in next ch and in next 17 sts) 4 times †, sc in next ch, repeat from † to † once; join with slip st to first sc, finish off.

PEBBLE BEACH Continued from page 88.

PEBBLE BEACH Continued from page 88.

EDGING

Rnd 1: Ch 1, turn; sc in first dc, ch 1, skip next ch, sc in next ch, ch 1, (skip next st, sc in next ch, ch 1) 3 times, skip next hdc, ★ sc in next hdc, ch 1, (skip next ch, sc in next st, ch 1) 6 times, skip next hdc, sc in next ch, ch 1, (skip next st, sc in next ch, ch 1) twice, skip next hdc; repeat from ★ across to last ch-2 sp, sc in next ch, ch 1, skip next ch, (sc, ch 2, sc) in last dc, ch 1; working in end of rows, skip first row, (sc in next row, ch 1) across; working in free loops of beginning ch *(Fig. 21b, page 142)*, (sc, ch 2, sc) in marked ch, ch 1, (skip next ch, sc in next ch, ch 1) across to last 2 chs, skip next ch, (sc, ch 2, sc) in last ch, ch 1; working in end of rows, skip first row, (sc in next row, ch 1) across, sc in same st as first sc, ch 2; join with slip st to first sc.

Rnd 2: Ch 1, do **not** turn; sc in same st, (ch 1, sc in next sc) across to next corner ch-2 sp, (sc, ch 2, sc) in corner ch-2 sp, ★ sc in next sc, (ch 1, sc in next sc) across to next corner ch-2 sp, (sc, ch 2, sc) in corner ch-2 sp; repeat from ★ 2 times **more**; join with slip st to first sc.

Rnd 3: Slip st in first ch-1 sp, ch 2, ★ (slip st in next ch-1 sp, ch 2) across to within 2 sc of next corner ch-2 sp, skip next sc, slip st in next sc, ch 2, slip st in corner ch-2 sp, ch 2, slip st in next sc, ch 2; repeat from ★ around; join with slip st to first slip st, finish off.

EBB AND FLOW Continued from page 90.

EBB AND FLOW Continued from page 90.

EDGING

Rnd 1: Ch 1, turn; slip st in first sc, ch 2, (slip st in next ch-1 sp, ch 2) across to last 2 sc, skip next sc, (slip st, ch 2) twice in last sc; working in end of rows, skip first row, ★ [(slip st in next row, ch 2) twice, skip next row] twice, slip st in next row, ch 2, skip next row; repeat from ★ across; working in sps and in free loops of beginning ch *(Fig. 21b, page 142)*, (slip st, ch 2) twice in ch at base of first sc, (slip st in next sp, ch 2) across to last 2 chs, skip next ch, (slip st, ch 2) twice in last ch; working in end of rows, skip first row, † slip st in next row, ch 2, skip next row, [(slip st in next row, ch 2) twice, skip next row] twice †; repeat from † to † across, slip st in same st as first slip st, ch 2; join with slip st to first slip st.

Rnd 2: Slip st in first ch-2 sp, ch 1, do **not** turn; sc in same sp, ch 1, ★ (sc in next ch-2 sp, ch 1) across to next corner ch-2 sp, (sc, ch 2, sc) in corner ch-2 sp, ch 1; repeat from ★ around; join with slip st to first sc.

Rnd 3: ★ (Slip st in next ch-1 sp, ch 2) across to next corner ch-2 sp, (slip st, ch 2) twice in corner ch-2 sp; repeat from ★ around to last ch-1 sp, slip st in last ch-1 sp, ch 2; join with slip st to first slip st, finish off.

CLIMBING VINES

Climbing like vines to the sunlight, stripes of deep green and blue come together to create a gorgeous combination on our cozy wrap. You'll enjoy stitching this afghan every bit as much as cuddling up with it!

Finished Size: 44" x 64"

MATERIALS
Worsted Weight Yarn:
Blue - 28 ounces,
(800 grams, 1,585 yards)
Ecru - 16 ounces,
(450 grams, 905 yards)
Green - 9 ounces,
(260 grams, 510 yards)
Crochet hook, size G (4.00 mm) **or** size
needed for gauge

GAUGE: In pattern, 12 dc = 4";
8 rows = 3¾"

Gauge Swatch: 5¼"w x 4¼"h
With Blue, ch 17 **loosely**.
Work same as Afghan for 9 rows.

Each row is worked across length of Afghan. When joining yarn and finishing off, always leave a 9" length to be worked into fringe.

AFGHAN

With Blue, ch 195 **loosely**.

Row 1: Working in back ridges of beginning ch *(Fig. 2b, page 139)*, 2 dc in fifth ch from hook, (skip next ch, 2 dc in next ch) across to last 2 chs, skip next ch, dc in last ch: 191 dc.

Row 2 (Right side)**:** Ch 3 **(counts as first dc, now and throughout)**, turn; skip next dc, 2 dc in sp **before** next dc *(Fig. 23, page 143)*, (skip next 2 dc, 2 dc in sp **before** next dc) across to last dc, skip last dc, dc in next ch: 192 dc.

Note: Loop a short piece of yarn around any stitch to mark Row 2 as **right** side.

Row 3: Ch 3, turn; skip next dc, 2 dc in sp **before** next dc, (skip next 2 dc, 2 dc in sp **before** next dc) across to last 2 dc, skip next dc, dc in last dc; finish off.

Row 4: With **right** side facing, join Ecru with slip st in first dc; ch 3, skip next dc, 2 dc in sp **before** next dc, (skip next 2 dc, 2 dc in sp **before** next dc) across to last 2 dc, skip next dc, dc in last dc; finish off.

Row 5: With **wrong** side facing, join Green with slip st in first dc; ch 3, skip next dc, 2 dc in sp **before** next dc, (skip next 2 dc, 2 dc in sp **before** next dc) across to last 2 dc, skip next dc, dc in last dc; finish off.

Row 6: Repeat Row 4.

Row 7: With **wrong** side facing, join Blue with slip st in first dc; ch 3, skip next dc, 2 dc in sp **before** next dc, (skip next 2 dc, 2 dc in sp **before** next dc) across to last 2 dc, skip next dc, dc in last dc.

Row 8: Ch 3, turn; skip next dc, 2 dc in sp **before** next dc, (skip next 2 dc, 2 dc in sp **before** next dc) across to last 2 dc, skip next dc, dc in last dc.

Row 9: Ch 3, turn; skip next dc, 2 dc in sp **before** next dc, (skip next 2 dc, 2 dc in sp **before** next dc) across to last 2 dc, skip next dc, dc in last dc; finish off.

Rows 10-93: Repeat Rows 4-9, 14 times.

Holding 10 strands of corresponding color together, each 18" long, and using photo as a guide for placement, add additional fringe in end of rows across short edges of Afghan *(Figs. 27b & d, page 143)*.

september

IVORY ELEGANCE

Exquisite in ivory, our toasty throw features rows of raised stitches that resemble chains of tiny hearts. What a fitting gift idea for a bridal shower or wedding anniversary!

Finished Size: 47" x 69"

MATERIALS
Worsted Weight Yarn:
    65 ounces, (1,850 grams, 4,235 yards)
    Crochet hook, size G (4.00 mm) **or** size needed
        for gauge

GAUGE: In pattern, 16 sts and 12 rows = 4$^1/_2$"

Gauge Swatch: 4$^1/_2$" square
Ch 17 **loosely**.
Work same as Afghan for 12 rows.
Finish off.

Each row is worked across length of Afghan.

AFGHAN
Ch 245 **loosely**.
Row 1: Hdc in back ridge of third ch from hook **(2 skipped chs count as first hdc)** and each ch across **(Fig. 2b, page 139)**: 244 hdc.
Row 2 (Right side)**:** Ch 1, turn; sc in Back Loop Only of each hdc across **(Fig. 20, page 142)**.
Note: Loop a short piece of yarn around any stitch to mark Row 2 as **right** side.
Row 3: Ch 3 **(counts as first dc, now and throughout)**, turn; working in both loops, dc in next sc, ★ skip next 3 sc, tr in next sc, working in **front** of tr just made, dc in 3 skipped sc; repeat from ★ across to last 2 sc, dc in last 2 sc.
Row 4: Ch 3, turn; dc in next dc, ★ skip next 3 dc, tr in next tr, working **behind** tr just made, dc in 3 skipped dc; repeat from ★ across to last 2 dc, dc in last 2 dc.
Row 5: Ch 1, turn; sc in each st across.
Rows 6 and 7: Ch 2 **(counts as first hdc, now and throughout)**, turn; hdc in Back Loop Only of next st and each st across.
Row 8: Ch 1, turn; sc in Back Loop Only of each hdc across.
Rows 9-126: Repeat Rows 3-8, 19 times; then repeat Rows 3-6 once **more**.
Finish off.

Holding 5 strands of yarn together, each 16" long, add fringe across short edges of Afghan **(Figs. 27b & d, page 143)**.

PLEASING PLAID

*Add warm, rustic appeal to your decor with our rich
fringed throw. Rust and green stripes cross to create the plaid
pattern, and long fringe adds a handsome finishing touch.*

Finished Size: 51" x 64"

MATERIALS
  Worsted Weight Yarn:
    Ecru - 42¼ ounces, (1,200 grams, 2,775 yards)
    Rust - 7 ounces, (200 grams, 460 yards)
    Green - 7 ounces, (200 grams, 460 yards)
  Crochet hook, size Q (15.00 mm)

Entire Afghan is worked holding two strands of yarn together.

GAUGE: In pattern, (ch 1, 4 sc) twice = 6½";
        8 rows = 5"

Gauge Swatch: 9"w x 5½"h
With Ecru, ch 15 **loosely**.
Work same as Afghan Body for 8 rows.
Finish off.

AFGHAN BODY
With Ecru, ch 80 **loosely**.
Row 1 (Right side): Sc in second ch from hook and in next
3 chs, (ch 1, skip next ch, sc in next 4 chs) across: 64 sc and
15 ch-1 sps.
Note: Loop a short piece of yarn around any stitch to mark
Row 1 as **right** side.
Rows 2 and 3: Ch 1, turn; sc in first 4 sc, (ch 1, sc in next
4 sc) across.
Row 4: Ch 1, turn; sc in first 4 sc, (ch 1, sc in next 4 sc) across
changing to Rust in last sc *(Fig. 22a, page 142)*.
Row 5: Ch 1, turn; sc in first 4 sc, (ch 1, sc in next 4 sc) across
changing to Ecru in last sc.
Rows 6-8: Ch 1, turn; sc in first 4 sc, (ch 1, sc in next 4 sc)
across.

Row 9: Ch 1, turn; sc in first 4 sc, (ch 1, sc in next 4 sc) across
changing to Green in last sc.
Row 10: Ch 1, turn; sc in first 4 sc, (ch 1, sc in next 4 sc)
across changing to Ecru in last sc.
Rows 11-13: Ch 1, turn; sc in first 4 sc, (ch 1, sc in next 4 sc)
across.
Repeat Rows 4-13 until Afghan Body measures approximately
63" from beginning ch; do **not** finish off.
Last Row: Ch 1, turn; sc in first 4 sc, (ch 1, sc in next 4 sc)
across; finish off.

VERTICAL STRIPES
When joining yarn and finishing off, leave a 9" end to be worked
into fringe.

Row 1: With **right** side facing, join Rust with slip st around first
skipped ch on beginning ch; working across rows, ★ slip st
around corresponding skipped ch on **next** row; repeat from ★
across; finish off.
Row 2: With **right** side facing, join Green with slip st around
next skipped ch on beginning ch; working across rows,
★ slip st around corresponding skipped ch on **next** row; repeat
from ★ across; finish off.
Row 3: With **right** side facing, join Rust with slip st around
next skipped ch on beginning ch; working across rows,
★ slip st around corresponding skipped ch on **next** row; repeat
from ★ across; finish off.
Rows 4-15: Repeat Rows 2 and 3, 6 times.

Using 6 strands of corresponding color, each 18" long, add
additional fringe in each st across short edges of Afghan
(Figs. 27a & c, page 143).

SAPPHIRE SEA

Lose yourself in a sea of serene blue when you wrap up in this deep sapphire afghan. Popcorn and cluster stitches lend texture to the lacy throw, and a ruffle-look trim adds an elegant finale.

Finished Size: 45" x 60"

MATERIALS
Worsted Weight Yarn:
35 1/2 ounces, (1,010 grams, 2,495 yards)
Crochet hook, size I (5.50 mm) **or** size needed for gauge

GAUGE: In pattern, one repeat = 4 1/2 "; 8 rows = 4"

Gauge Swatch: 5 1/4 "w x 4"h
Ch 23 **loosely**.
Work same as Afghan Body for 8 rows.
Finish off.

STITCH GUIDE

RIGHT SIDE POPCORN
5 Dc in sp indicated, drop loop from hook, insert hook from **front** to **back** in first dc of 5-dc group, hook dropped loop and draw through.

WRONG SIDE POPCORN
5 Dc in sp indicated, drop loop from hook, insert hook from **back** to **front** in first dc of 5-dc group pushing sts to **right** side, hook dropped loop and draw through.

CLUSTER
★ YO twice, insert hook in st indicated, YO and pull up a loop, (YO and draw through 2 loops on hook) twice; repeat from ★ once **more**, YO and draw through all 3 loops on hook *(Figs. 15a & b, page 141)*.

AFGHAN BODY

Ch 167 **loosely**.

Row 1: Dc in fourth ch from hook **(3 skipped chs count as first dc)** and in next ch, ★ skip next ch, (dc, ch 1, dc) in next ch, [skip next 2 chs, (dc, ch 1, dc) in next ch] 4 times, skip next ch, dc in next 3 chs; repeat from ★ across: 120 dc and 45 ch-1 sps.

Row 2 (Right side)**:** Ch 3 **(counts as first dc, now and throughout)**, turn; dc in next 2 dc, ★ (dc, ch 1, dc) in next ch-1 sp, ch 5, skip next ch-1 sp, sc in next ch-1 sp, ch 5, skip next ch-1 sp, (dc, ch 1, dc) in next ch-1 sp, skip next dc, dc in next 3 dc; repeat from ★ across: 66 dc and 36 sps.

Row 3: Ch 3, turn; dc in next 2 dc, ★ (dc, ch 1, dc) in next ch-1 sp, ch 3, (sc in next ch-5 sp, ch 3) twice, (dc, ch 1, dc) in next ch-1 sp, skip next dc, dc in next 3 dc; repeat from ★ across: 66 dc and 45 sps.

Row 4: Ch 3, turn; dc in next 2 dc, ★ (dc, ch 1, dc) in next ch-1 sp, skip next ch-3 sp, work right side Popcorn in next ch-3 sp, (ch 2, work right side Popcorn in same sp) twice, (dc, ch 1, dc) in next ch-1 sp, skip next dc, dc in next 3 dc; repeat from ★ across: 27 right side Popcorns.

Row 5: Ch 3, turn; dc in next 2 dc, ★ (dc, ch 1, dc) in next ch-1 sp, ch 3, skip next 2 sts, (sc in next ch-2 sp, ch 3) twice, (dc, ch 1, dc) in next ch-1 sp, skip next dc, dc in next 3 dc; repeat from ★ across: 66 dc and 45 sps.

Row 6: Ch 3, turn; dc in next 2 dc, ★ (dc, ch 1, dc) in next ch-1 sp, (dc, ch 1, dc) in next 3 ch-3 sps and in next ch-1 sp, skip next dc, dc in next 3 dc; repeat from ★ across: 120 dc and 45 ch-1 sps.

Continued on page 107.

PLAYTIME GRANNY

*Bursting with the bright colors kids love, our playtime granny
is ideal for warming up little ones. Perky cluster stitches and
scalloped edging surround the afghan, giving it a "bubbly" trim.*

Finished Size: 37" x 45"

MATERIALS
Sport Weight Yarn:
Yellow - 14 ounces, (400 grams, 1,120 yards)
Red - 6 ounces, (170 grams, 480 yards)
Blue - 4³/4 ounces, (130 grams, 380 yards)
Crochet hook, size G (4.00 mm) **or** size needed
for gauge
Yarn needle

GAUGE SWATCH: 4"
Work same as Square A, B, or C.

STITCH GUIDE

CLUSTER (uses one ch-3 sp)
★ YO, insert hook in ch-3-sp indicated, YO and pull up a
loop, YO and draw through 2 loops on hook; repeat from ★
once **more**, YO and draw through all 3 loops on hook
(Figs. 15a & b, page 141).
SCALLOP
Ch 3, dc in third ch from hook.

SQUARE A (Make 27)
Rnd 1 (Right side): With Blue, ch 4, 2 dc in fourth ch from
hook, ch 3, (3 dc in same ch, ch 3) 3 times; join with slip st to
top of beginning ch-4, finish off: 4 ch-3 sps.
Note: Loop a short piece of yarn around any stitch to mark
Rnd 1 as **right** side.
Rnd 2: With **right** side facing, join Red with slip st in any
ch-3 sp; ch 3 **(counts as first dc, now and throughout)**,
(2 dc, ch 3, 3 dc) in same sp, ch 1, ★ (3 dc, ch 3, 3 dc) in next
ch-3 sp, ch 1; repeat from ★ 2 times **more**; join with slip st to
first dc, finish off: 24 dc and 8 sps.

Rnd 3: With **right** side facing, join Yellow with slip st in any
ch-3 sp; ch 3, (2 dc, ch 3, 3 dc) in same sp, ch 1, 3 dc in next
ch-1 sp, ch 1, ★ (3 dc, ch 3, 3 dc) in next ch-3 sp, ch 1, 3 dc in
next ch-1 sp, ch 1; repeat from ★ 2 times **more**; join with slip st
to first dc, do **not** finish off: 36 dc and 12 sps.
Rnd 4: Slip st in next 2 dc and in next ch-3 sp, ch 3, (2 dc,
ch 3, 3 dc) in same sp, ch 1, (3 dc in next ch-1 sp, ch 1) twice,
★ (3 dc, ch 3, 3 dc) in next ch-3 sp, ch 1, (3 dc in next ch-1 sp,
ch 1) twice; repeat from ★ 2 times **more**; join with slip st to
first dc, finish off: 48 dc and 16 sps.

SQUARE B (Make 27)
Rnd 1 (Right side): With Red, ch 4, 2 dc in fourth ch from
hook, ch 3, (3 dc in same ch, ch 3) 3 times; join with slip st to
top of beginning ch-4, finish off: 4 ch-3 sps.
Note: Mark Rnd 1 as **right** side.
Rnd 2: With **right** side facing, join Yellow with slip st in any
ch-3 sp; ch 3, (2 dc, ch 3, 3 dc) in same sp, ch 1, ★ (3 dc,
ch 3, 3 dc) in next ch-3 sp, ch 1; repeat from ★ 2 times **more**;
join with slip st to first dc, finish off: 24 dc and 8 sps.
Rnd 3: With **right** side facing, join Blue with slip st in any
ch-3 sp; ch 3, (2 dc, ch 3, 3 dc) in same sp, ch 1, 3 dc in next
ch-1 sp, ch 1, ★ (3 dc, ch 3, 3 dc) in next ch-3 sp, ch 1, 3 dc in
next ch-1 sp, ch 1; repeat from ★ 2 times **more**; join with slip st
to first dc, finish off: 36 dc and 12 sps.
Rnd 4: With **right** side facing, join Yellow with slip st in any
ch-3 sp; ch 3, (2 dc, ch 3, 3 dc) in same sp, ch 1, (3 dc in next
ch-1 sp, ch 1) twice, ★ (3 dc, ch 3, 3 dc) in next ch-3 sp, ch 1,
(3 dc in next ch-1 sp, ch 1) twice; repeat from ★ 2 times **more**;
join with slip st to first dc, finish off: 48 dc and 16 sps.

Continued on page 106.

SQUARE C (Make 26)

Rnd 1 (Right side)**:** With Yellow, ch 4, 2 dc in fourth ch from hook, ch 3, (3 dc in same ch, ch 3) 3 times; join with slip st to top of beginning ch-4, finish off: 4 ch-3 sps.

Note: Mark Rnd 1 as **right** side.

Rnd 2: With **right** side facing, join Blue with slip st in any ch-3 sp; ch 3, (2 dc, ch 3, 3 dc) in same sp, ch 1, ★ (3 dc, ch 3, 3 dc) in next ch-3 sp, ch 1; repeat from ★ 2 times **more**; join with slip st to first dc, finish off: 24 dc and 8 sps.

Rnd 3: With **right** side facing, join Red with slip st in any ch-3 sp; ch 3, (2 dc, ch 3, 3 dc) in same sp, ch 1, 3 dc in next ch-1 sp, ch 1, ★ (3 dc, ch 3, 3 dc) in next ch-3 sp, ch 1, 3 dc in next ch-1 sp, ch 1; repeat from ★ 2 times **more**; join with slip st to first dc, finish off: 36 dc and 12 sps.

Rnd 4: With **right** side facing, join Yellow with slip st in any ch-3 sp; ch 3, (2 dc, ch 3, 3 dc) in same sp, ch 1, (3 dc in next ch-1 sp, ch 1) twice, ★ (3 dc, ch 3, 3 dc) in next ch-3 sp, ch 1, (3 dc in next ch-1 sp, ch 1) twice; repeat from ★ 2 times **more**; join with slip st to first dc, finish off: 48 dc and 16 sps.

ASSEMBLY

With Yellow, using Placement Diagram as a guide, and working though both loops, whipstitch Squares together *(Fig. 26b, page 143)*, forming 8 vertical strips of 10 Squares each, beginning in center ch of first corner ch-3 and ending in center ch of next corner ch-3; whipstitch strips together in same manner.

PLACEMENT DIAGRAM

A	B	C	A	B	C	A	B
C	A	B	C	A	B	C	A
B	C	A	B	C	A	B	C
A	B	C	A	B	C	A	B
C	A	B	C	A	B	C	A
B	C	A	B	C	A	B	C
A	B	C	A	B	C	A	B
C	A	B	C	A	B	C	A
B	C	A	B	C	A	B	C
A	B	C	A	B	C	A	B

EDGING

Rnd 1: With **right** side facing, join Yellow with sc in any corner ch-3 sp *(see Joining With Sc, page 142)*; ch 2, sc in same sp, ★ † ch 1, skip next dc, sc in next dc, ch 1, (sc in next ch-1 sp, ch 1, skip next dc, sc in next dc, ch 1) 3 times, **[**(sc in next sp, ch 1) twice, skip next dc, sc in next dc, ch 1, (sc in next ch-1 sp, ch 1, skip next dc, sc in next dc, ch 1) 3 times**]** across to next corner ch-3 sp †, (sc, ch 2, sc) in corner ch-3 sp; repeat from ★ 2 times **more**, then repeat from † to † once; join with slip st to first sc: 324 sps.

Rnds 2 and 3: Ch 1, (sc, ch 2, sc) in first corner ch-2 sp, ch 1, (sc in next ch-1 sp, ch 1) across to next corner ch-2 sp, ★ (sc, ch 2, sc) in corner ch-2 sp, ch 1, (sc in next ch-1 sp, ch 1) across to next corner ch-2 sp; repeat from ★ 2 times **more**; join with slip st to first sc: 332 sps. Finish off.

Rnd 4: With **right** side facing, join Red with slip st in any corner ch-2 sp; ch 3, (2 dc, ch 3, 3 dc) in same sp, ch 1, skip next ch-1 sp, (3 dc in next ch-1 sp, ch 1, skip next ch-1 sp) across to next corner ch-2 sp, ★ (3 dc, ch 3, 3 dc) in corner ch-2 sp, ch 1, skip next ch-1 sp, (3 dc in next ch-1 sp, ch 1, skip next ch-1 sp) across to next corner ch-2 sp; repeat from ★ 2 times **more**; join with slip st to first dc, finish off: 170 sps.

Rnd 5: With **right** side facing, join Blue with slip st in any corner ch-3 sp; ch 3, (2 dc, ch 3, 3 dc) in same sp, ch 1, (3 dc in next ch-1 sp, ch 1) across to next corner ch-3 sp, ★ (3 dc, ch 3, 3 dc) in corner ch-3 sp, ch 1, (3 dc in next ch-1 sp, ch 1) across to next corner ch-3 sp; repeat from ★ 2 times **more**; join with slip st to first dc, finish off: 174 sps.

Rnd 6: With **right** side facing, join Red with slip st in any corner ch-3 sp; ch 3, (2 dc, ch 3, 3 dc) in same sp, ch 1, (3 dc in next ch-1 sp, ch 1) across to next corner ch-3 sp, ★ (3 dc, ch 3, 3 dc) in corner ch-3 sp, ch 1, (3 dc in next ch-1 sp, ch 1) across to next corner ch-3 sp; repeat from ★ 2 times **more**; join with slip st to first dc, finish off: 178 sps.

Rnd 7: With **right** side facing, join Yellow with slip st in any corner ch-3 sp; ch 3, (2 dc, ch 3, 3 dc) in same sp, ch 1, (3 dc in next ch-1 sp, ch 1) across to next corner ch-3 sp, ★ (3 dc, ch 3, 3 dc) in corner ch-3 sp, ch 1, (3 dc in next ch-1 sp, ch 1) across to next corner ch-3 sp; repeat from ★ 2 times **more**; join with slip st to first dc, do **not** finish off: 182 sps.

Rnd 8: Slip st in next 2 dc, ★ (slip st, ch 2, work Cluster, ch 2, slip st) in next corner ch-3 sp, work Scallop, (slip st in next ch-1 sp, work Scallop) across to next corner ch-3 sp; repeat from ★ around; join with slip st to slip st at base of beginning ch-2, finish off.

Row 7: Ch 3, turn; dc in next 2 dc, ★ (dc, ch 1, dc) in next ch-1 sp, ch 5, skip next ch-1 sp, sc in next ch-1 sp, ch 5, skip next ch-1 sp, (dc, ch 1, dc) in next ch-1 sp, skip next dc, dc in next 3 dc; repeat from ★ across: 66 dc and 36 sps.

Row 8: Ch 3, turn; dc in next 2 dc, ★ (dc, ch 1, dc) in next ch-1 sp, ch 3, (sc in next ch-5 sp, ch 3) twice, (dc, ch 1, dc) in next ch-1 sp, skip next dc, dc in next 3 dc; repeat from ★ across: 66 dc and 45 sps.

Row 9: Ch 3, turn; dc in next 2 dc, ★ (dc, ch 1, dc) in next ch-1 sp, skip next ch-3 sp, work wrong side Popcorn in next ch-3 sp, (ch 2, work wrong side Popcorn in same sp) twice, (dc, ch 1, dc) in next ch-1 sp, skip next dc, dc in next 3 dc; repeat from ★ across: 27 wrong side Popcorns.

Row 10: Ch 3, turn; dc in next 2 dc, ★ (dc, ch 1, dc) in next ch-1 sp, ch 3, skip next 2 sts, (sc in next ch-2 sp, ch 3) twice, (dc, ch 1, dc) in next ch-1 sp, skip next dc, dc in next 3 dc; repeat from ★ across: 66 dc and 45 sps.

Row 11: Ch 3, turn; dc in next 2 dc, ★ (dc, ch 1, dc) in next ch-1 sp, (dc, ch 1, dc) in next 3 ch-3 sps and in next ch-1 sp, skip next dc, dc in next 3 dc; repeat from ★ across: 120 dc and 45 ch-1 sps.

Rows 12-111: Repeat Rows 2-11, 10 times; at end of last row, do **not** finish off.

EDGING

Rnd 1: Ch 1, turn; 2 sc in first dc, work 161 sc evenly spaced across to last dc, 3 sc in last dc; work 221 sc evenly spaced across end of rows; working in free loops of beginning ch *(Fig. 21b, page 142)*, 3 sc in ch at base of first dc, work 161 sc evenly spaced across to last ch, 3 sc in last ch; work 221 sc evenly spaced across end of rows, sc in same st as first sc; join with slip st to first sc: 776 sc.

Rnd 2: Ch 4, turn; dc in same st, ch 1, skip next sc, ★ (dc in next sc, ch 1, skip next sc) across to center sc of next corner 3-sc group, (dc, ch 1) twice in center sc, skip next sc; repeat from ★ 2 times **more**, (dc in next sc, ch 1, skip next sc) across; join with slip st to third ch of beginning ch-4: 392 ch-1 sps.

Rnd 3: Ch 3, turn; (tr, ch 2, work Cluster) in same st, [skip next dc, work (Cluster, ch 2, Cluster) in next dc] across to next corner ch-1 sp, ★ work (Cluster, ch 2, Cluster) in next dc, [skip next dc, work (Cluster, ch 2, Cluster) in next dc] across to next corner ch-1 sp; repeat from ★ 2 times **more**; join with slip st to first tr: 199 ch-2 sps.

Rnd 4: Ch 1, turn; sc in same st, ch 4, (sc in next 2 Clusters, ch 4) around to last Cluster, sc in last Cluster; join with slip st to first sc, finish off.

MARVELOUS MOSAIC

Simple chains and single crochets are coupled with variegated yarn in vivid jewel tones to create the rich mosaic weave in this cozy wrap. Doesn't it look marvelous paired with a plain coverlet?

AFGHAN BODY

Ch 90 **loosely**.

Row 1 (Right side)**:** Sc in second ch from hook, ★ ch 1, skip next ch, sc in next ch; repeat from ★ across: 45 sc and 44 ch-1 sps.

Row 2: Ch 1, turn; sc in first sc and next ch-1 sp, (ch 1, sc in next ch-1 sp) across to last sc, sc in last sc: 46 sc and 43 ch-1 sps.

Row 3: Ch 1, turn; sc in first sc, ch 1, (sc in next ch-1 sp, ch 1) across to last 2 sc, skip next sc, sc in last sc: 45 sc and 44 ch-1 sps.

Rows 4-123: Repeat Rows 2 and 3, 60 times; do **not** finish off.

EDGING

Rnd 1: Ch 1, do **not** turn; sc in end of each row across; working in ch-1 sps and in free loops of beginning ch *(Fig. 21b, page 142)*, 3 sc in first ch, sc in next ch-1 sp, (sc in next ch and in next ch-1 sp) across, 3 sc in next ch; sc in end of each row across; working in sts on Row 123, 3 sc in first sc, sc in each ch-1 sp and in each sc across to last sc, 3 sc in last sc; join with slip st to first sc: 432 sc.

Rnd 2: Slip st in next sc, ch 1, sc in same st, ch 3, sc in second ch from hook, ch 1, skip next sc, ★ sc in next sc, ch 3, sc in second ch from hook, ch 1, skip next st; repeat from ★ around; join with slip st to first sc, finish off.

Finished Size: 53" x 72"

MATERIALS
Variegated Worsted Weight Yarn:
66 ounces,
(1,870 grams, 3,830 yards)
Crochet hook, size Q (15.00 mm)

Afghan is worked holding two strands of yarn together.

GAUGE: In pattern, (sc, ch 1) 4 times and 8 rows = 4¹/₂ "

Gauge Swatch: 5"w x 4¹/₂ "h
Ch 10 **loosely**.
Work same as Afghan for 8 rows.
Finish off.

SERENE WRAP

When spending a quiet moment away from your busy day, you can reach for this plush afghan with its soothing hue. The wrap features cluster-stitch panels that alternate with rows featuring V-shapes for a texture that's very appealing.

Finished Size: 49" x 63"

MATERIALS
Worsted Weight Yarn:
72 ounces, (2,040 grams, 4,070 yards)
Crochet hook, size H (5.00 mm) **or** size needed
for gauge
Yarn needle

GAUGE: Panel A = 2³/4" wide
In pattern, 7 sc = 2"; 3 sc rows = ³/4"
Panel B = 8¹/2" wide
In pattern, 8 Clusters and 9 rows = 5"

Gauge Swatch: 4" w x 2³/4" h
Ch 15 **loosely.**
Rows 1-8: Work same as Panel A.
Finish off.

STITCH GUIDE

CLUSTER
First Leg: YO, insert hook in ch indicated, YO and pull up a loop, YO, insert hook in same ch, YO and pull up a loop (5 loops on hook).
Second Leg: YO, insert hook in ch indicated, YO and pull up a loop, YO, insert hook in same ch, YO and pull up a loop, YO and draw through all 9 loops on hook.

PANEL A (Make 5)

Each row is worked across length of Panel.
Ch 219 **loosely.**
Row 1 (Right side)**:** Sc in back ridge of second ch from hook and each ch across *(Fig. 2b, page 139)*: 218 sc.
Note: Loop a short piece of yarn around first sc made to mark Row 1 as **right** side and to mark bottom edge.
Rows 2 and 3: Ch 1, turn; sc in each sc across.
Row 4: Ch 3 **(counts as first dc, now and throughout)**, turn; ★ skip next 3 sc, tr in next sc, working in **front** of tr just made and inserting hook from **back** to **front**, dc in 3 skipped sc; repeat from ★ across to last sc, dc in last sc.

Row 5: Ch 3, turn; ★ skip next 3 dc, tr in next tr, working **behind** tr just made and inserting hook from **front** to **back**, dc in 3 skipped dc; repeat from ★ across to last dc, dc in last dc; finish off.
Row 6: With **right** side facing, join yarn with sc in first dc *(see Joining With Sc, page 142)*; sc in next tr and in each st across.
Rows 7 and 8: Ch 1, turn; sc in each sc across. Finish off.

PANEL B (Make 4)

Ch 42 **loosely.**
Row 1 (Right side)**:** Work First Leg of Cluster in third ch from hook, skip next 2 chs, work Second Leg of Cluster in next ch, ★ ch 1, work First Leg of Cluster in same ch as Second Leg of Cluster just made, skip next 2 chs, work Second Leg of Cluster in next ch; repeat from ★ across: 13 Clusters.
Note: Loop a short piece of yarn around any stitch to mark Row 1 as **right** side and bottom edge.
Row 2: Ch 3, turn; work First Leg of Cluster in third ch from hook, skip first Cluster, work Second Leg of Cluster in next ch, ★ ch 1, work First Leg of Cluster in same ch as Second Leg of Cluster just made, skip next Cluster, work Second Leg of Cluster in next ch; repeat from ★ across working Second Leg of last Cluster in top of turning ch.
Repeat Row 2 until Panel B is the same length as Panel A, ending last row with a ch-1 to close; finish off.

ASSEMBLY

Alternating Panels and beginning and ending with Panel A, lay out Panels with **right** sides facing and marked edges at same end; sew Panels together *(Fig. 25, page 143)*.

EDGING

With **right** side facing, join yarn with sc in any st; sc evenly around entire Afghan working 3 sc in each corner; join with slip st to first sc, finish off.

Holding 4 strands of yarn together, each 16" long, add fringe across short edges of Afghan *(Figs. 27a & c, page 143)*.

COLORFUL COVERLET

This captivating spread is perfect for brightening any room in the house. Pull out your yarn scraps to make the multicolored hexagon motifs, which look positively splendid joined with black.

Finished Size: 44" x 58"

MATERIALS
Worsted Weight Yarn:
    Black - 26 ounces, (740 grams, 1,470 yards)
    Scraps - 21 ounces, (600 grams, 1,190 yards) **total**
        Note: We used 16 different colors. One Motif
          requires 10 yards.
Crochet hook, size I (5.50 mm) **or** size needed
    for gauge
Yarn needle

GAUGE: Each Motif = 4³/₄" (straight edge to straight edge)

Gauge Swatch: 3³/₄"
Work same as Motif through Rnd 3.

STITCH GUIDE

> **LONG DOUBLE CROCHET** *(abbreviated LDC)*
> YO, working **around** ch-1 on previous 2 rnds, insert hook
> in sp indicated, YO and pull up a loop even with last st made,
> (YO and draw through 2 loops on hook) twice *(Fig. 9,*
> *page 140)*.
> **DECREASE** (uses next 2 sps)
> ★ YO, insert hook in **next** sp, YO and pull up a loop, YO and
> draw through 2 loops on hook; repeat from ★ once **more**,
> YO and draw through all 3 loops on hook.

MOTIF (Make 111)
With Scrap color desired, ch 4; join with slip st to form a ring.
Rnd 1 (Right side)**:** Ch 3 **(counts as first dc, now and**
throughout), dc in ring, ch 2, (2 dc in ring, ch 2) 5 times; join
with slip st to first dc: 12 dc and 6 ch-2 sps.
Note: Loop a short piece of yarn around any stitch to mark
Rnd 1 as **right** side.
Rnd 2: Slip st in next dc and in next ch-2 sp, ch 3, (dc, ch 2,
2 dc) in same sp, ch 1, ★ (2 dc, ch 2, 2 dc) in next ch-2 sp,
ch 1; repeat from ★ around; join with slip st to first dc: 24 dc
and 12 sps.

Rnd 3: Ch 3, dc in next dc, (dc, ch 2, dc) in next ch-2 sp, dc in
next 2 dc, ch 1, skip next ch-1 sp, ★ dc in next 2 dc, (dc, ch 2,
dc) in next ch-2 sp, dc in next 2 dc, ch 1, skip next ch-1 sp;
repeat from ★ around; join with slip st to first dc, finish off:
36 dc and 12 sps.
Rnd 4: With **right** side facing, join Black with slip st in any
ch-2 sp; ch 6, dc in same sp and in next 3 dc, skip first dc of
next 2-dc group on Rnd 1, work LDC in sp **before** next dc, dc
in next 3 dc on Rnd 3, ★ (dc, ch 3, dc) in next ch-2 sp, dc in
next 3 dc, skip first dc of next 2-dc group on Rnd 1, work LDC
in sp **before** next dc, dc in next 3 dc on Rnd 3; repeat from ★
around; join with slip st to third ch of beginning ch-6, finish off:
54 sts and 6 ch-3 sps.

HALF MOTIF (Make 12)
With Scrap color desired, ch 4; join with slip st to form a ring.
Row 1 (Right side)**:** Ch 4 **(counts as first dc plus ch 1)**,
2 dc in ring, (ch 2, 2 dc in ring) twice, ch 1, dc in ring: 8 dc
and 4 sps.
Note: Mark Row 1 as **right** side.
Row 2: Ch 3, turn; dc in next ch-1 sp, ch 1, ★ (2 dc, ch 2,
2 dc) in next ch-2 sp, ch 1; repeat from ★ once **more**, dc in
next ch-1 sp and in last dc: 12 dc and 5 sps.
Row 3: Ch 3, turn; dc in same st and in next dc, ch 1, skip next
ch-1 sp, ★ dc in next 2 dc, (dc, ch 2, dc) in next ch-2 sp, dc in
next 2 dc, ch 1, skip next ch-1 sp; repeat from ★ once **more**,
dc in next dc, 2 dc in last dc, finish off: 18 dc and 5 sps.
Row 4: With **right** side facing, join Black with slip st in first dc;
ch 3, dc in same st and in next 2 dc, skip first dc of next
2-dc group on Row 1, work LDC in sp **before** next dc, ★ dc in
next 3 dc on Row 3, (dc, ch 3, dc) in next ch-2 sp, dc in next
3 dc, skip first dc of next 2-dc group on Row 1, work LDC in sp
before next dc; repeat from ★ once **more**, dc in next 2 dc on
Row 3, 2 dc in last dc; finish off: 27 sts and 2 ch-3 sps.

Continued on page 119.

113

DUTCH ROSE

*This stylish coverlet has all the charm of a hand-pieced quilt!
We worked the traditional Dutch Rose pattern in squares of deep
red and green to capture the colorful hues of autumn.*

Finished Size: 58" x 70"

MATERIALS

Worsted Weight Yarn:
　Tan - 40 ounces, (1,140 grams, 2,515 yards)
　Red - 14 ounces, (400 grams, 880 yards)
　Green - 3¹/₂ ounces, (100 grams, 220 yards)
　Lt Green - ³/₄ ounce, (20 grams, 45 yards)
Crochet hook, size I (5.50 mm) **or** size needed
　for gauge
Yarn needle

GAUGE SWATCH: 3"
Work same as Square A.

Referring to the Key, page 119, make the number of Squares specified in the colors indicated.

SQUARE A

With color indicated, ch 4; join with slip st to form a ring.
Rnd 1 (Right side)**:** Ch 3 (**counts as first dc, now and throughout**), 2 dc in ring, ch 2, (3 dc in ring, ch 2) 3 times; join with slip st to first dc: 12 dc and 4 ch-2 sps.
Note: Loop a short piece of yarn around any stitch to mark Rnd 1 as **right** side.
Rnd 2: Slip st in next 2 dc and in next ch-2 sp, ch 3, (2 dc, ch 2, 3 dc) in same sp, ch 1, ★ (3 dc, ch 2, 3 dc) in next ch-2 sp, ch 1; repeat from ★ 2 times **more**; join with slip st to first dc, finish off: 24 dc and 8 sps.

SQUARE B

With first color indicated, ch 4; join with slip st to form a ring.
Rnd 1 (Right side)**:** Ch 5 (**counts as first dc plus ch 2**), 3 dc in ring, cut first color, with second color indicated, YO and draw through, ch 1, 3 dc in ring, ch 2, 3 dc in ring, cut second color, with first color, YO and draw through, ch 1, 2 dc in ring; join with slip st to first dc: 12 dc and 4 ch-2 sps.
Note: Mark Rnd 1 as **right** side.

Rnd 2: Slip st in first ch-2 sp, ch 3, (2 dc, ch 2, 3 dc) in same sp, ch 1, 3 dc in next ch-2 sp, cut first color, with second color, YO and draw through, ch 1, 3 dc in same sp, ch 1, (3 dc, ch 2, 3 dc) in next ch-2 sp, ch 1, 3 dc in next ch-2 sp, cut second color, with first color, YO and draw through, ch 1, 3 dc in same sp, ch 1; join with slip st to first dc, finish off: 24 dc and 8 sps.

ASSEMBLY

With matching color as desired, using Placement Diagram as a guide, and working through inside loops only, whipstitch Squares together (*Fig. 26a, page 143*), forming 18 vertical strips of 22 Squares each, beginning in second ch of first corner ch-2 and ending in first ch of next corner ch-2; whipstitch strips together in same manner.

EDGING

Rnd 1: With **right** side facing, join Tan with sc in any corner ch-2 sp (*see Joining With Sc, page 142*); (sc in next 3 dc and in next sp) twice, hdc in joining, (sc in next sp and in next 3 dc) twice, [sc in next sp, hdc in joining, (sc in next sp and in next 3 dc) twice] across to next corner ch-2 sp, ★ (sc, ch 2, sc) in corner ch-2 sp, (sc in next 3 dc and in next sp) twice, hdc in joining, (sc in next sp and in next 3 dc) twice, [sc in next sp, hdc in joining, (sc in next sp and in next 3 dc) twice] across to next corner ch-2 sp; repeat from ★ 2 times **more**, sc in same sp as first sc, ch 1, sc in first sc to form last ch-2 sp: 796 sts and 4 ch-2 sps.
Rnd 2: Ch 3, 2 dc in same sp, dc in each st across to next corner ch-2 sp, ★ (3 dc, ch 2, 3 dc) in corner ch-2 sp, dc in each st across to next corner ch-2 sp; repeat from ★ 2 times **more**, 3 dc in same sp as first dc, ch 1, sc in first dc to form last ch-2 sp: 820 dc and 4 ch-2 sps.
Rnd 3: Ch 4, skip next dc, (dc in next dc, ch 1, skip next dc) across to next corner ch-2 sp, ★ (dc, ch 2, dc) in corner ch-2 sp, ch 1, skip next dc, (dc in next dc, ch 1, skip next dc) across to next corner ch-2 sp; repeat from ★ 2 times **more**, dc in same sp as beginning ch-4, ch 1, sc in third ch of beginning ch-4 to form last ch-2 sp: 416 sts and 416 sps.

Continued on page 119.

HARVEST GOLD

Resembling rows of gracefully swaying wheat, chain loops accent this golden throw. The illusion of movement is enhanced by the elongated fringe.

Finished Size: 51" x 69"

MATERIALS
Worsted Weight Yarn:
  64 ounces, (1,820 grams, 3,735 yards)
  Crochet hook, size J (6.00 mm) **or** size needed
    for gauge

GAUGE: In pattern, 13 dc and 10 rows = 4"

Gauge Swatch: 4" square
Ch 15 **loosely**.

Row 1: Dc in fourth ch from hook **(3 skipped chs count as first dc)** and in each ch across: 13 dc.

Row 2: Ch 1, turn; sc in each dc across.

Row 3: Ch 3 **(counts as first dc)**, turn; dc in next sc and in each sc across.

Rows 4-10: Repeat Rows 2 and 3, 3 times; then repeat Row 2 once **more**.
Finish off.

STITCH GUIDE

> **CHAIN LOOP** *(abbreviated Ch Loop)*
> Insert hook in next dc, YO and pull up a loop, (YO and draw through one loop on hook) 8 times, YO and draw through both loops on hook **(counts as one st)**.

AFGHAN
Ch 167 **loosely**.

Row 1: Dc in fourth ch from hook **(3 skipped chs count as first dc)** and in each ch across: 165 dc.

Row 2 (Right side): Ch 1, turn; sc in first 15 dc, ★ work Ch Loop, (sc in next 3 dc, work Ch Loop) twice, sc in next 21 dc; repeat from ★ across: 15 Ch Loops.

Note: Loop a short piece of yarn around any stitch to mark Row 2 as **right** side.

Row 3: Ch 3 **(counts as first dc, now and throughout)**, turn; keeping Ch Loops to **back** of work, dc in next sc and in each st across.

To twist Ch Loop, turn Ch Loop toward the **right**.

Row 4: Ch 1, turn; sc in first 15 dc, ★ sc in next dc working **around** twisted Ch Loop, work Ch Loop, (sc in next 2 dc, sc in next dc working **around** twisted Ch Loop, work Ch Loop) twice, sc in next 20 dc; repeat from ★ across.

Row 5: Ch 3, turn; keeping Ch Loops to **back** of work, dc in next sc and in each st across.

Row 6: Ch 1, turn; sc in first 16 dc, sc in next dc working **around** twisted Ch Loop, work Ch Loop, (sc in next 2 dc, sc in next dc working **around** twisted Ch Loop, work Ch Loop) twice, ★ sc in next 20 dc, sc in next dc working **around** twisted Ch Loop, work Ch Loop, (sc in next 2 dc, sc in next dc working **around** twisted Ch Loop, work Ch Loop) twice; repeat from ★ across to last 19 dc, sc in last 19 dc.

Row 7: Ch 3, turn; keeping Ch Loops to **back** of work, dc in next sc and in each st across.

Row 8: Ch 1, turn; sc in first 17 dc, sc in next dc working **around** twisted Ch Loop, work Ch Loop, (sc in next 2 dc, sc in next dc working **around** twisted Ch Loop, work Ch Loop) twice, ★ sc in next 20 dc, sc in next dc working **around** twisted Ch Loop, work Ch Loop, (sc in next 2 dc, sc in next dc working **around** twisted Ch Loop, work Ch Loop) twice; repeat from ★ across to last 18 dc, sc in last 18 dc.

Row 9: Ch 3, turn; keeping Ch Loops to **back** of work, dc in next sc and in each st across.

Row 10: Ch 1, turn; sc in first 18 dc, sc in next dc working **around** twisted Ch Loop, work Ch Loop, (sc in next 2 dc, sc in next dc working **around** twisted Ch Loop, work Ch Loop) twice, ★ sc in next 20 dc, sc in next dc working **around** twisted Ch Loop, work Ch Loop, (sc in next 2 dc, sc in next dc working **around** twisted Ch Loop, work Ch Loop) twice; repeat from ★ across to last 17 dc, sc in last 17 dc.

Row 11: Ch 3, turn; keeping Ch Loops to **back** of work, dc in next sc and in each st across.

Continued on page 118.

Row 12: Ch 1, turn; sc in first 19 dc, sc in next dc working **around** twisted Ch Loop, work Ch Loop, (sc in next 2 dc, sc in next dc working **around** twisted Ch Loop, work Ch Loop) twice, ★ sc in next 20 dc, sc in next dc working **around** twisted Ch Loop, work Ch Loop, (sc in next 2 dc, sc in next dc working **around** twisted Ch Loop, work Ch Loop) twice; repeat from ★ across to last 16 dc, sc in last 16 dc.

Row 13: Ch 3, turn; keeping Ch Loops to **back** of work, dc in next sc and in each st across.

Row 14: Ch 1, turn; sc in first 20 dc, sc in next dc working **around** twisted Ch Loop, work Ch Loop, (sc in next 2 dc, sc in next dc working **around** twisted Ch Loop, work Ch Loop) twice, ★ sc in next 20 dc, sc in next dc working **around** twisted Ch Loop, work Ch Loop, (sc in next 2 dc, sc in next dc working **around** twisted Ch Loop, work Ch Loop) twice; repeat from ★ across to last 15 dc, sc in last 15 dc.

Row 15: Ch 3, turn; keeping Ch Loops to **back** of work, dc in next sc and in each st across.

Row 16: Ch 1, turn; sc in first 20 dc, work Ch Loop, sc in next dc working **around** twisted Ch Loop, (sc in next 2 dc, work Ch Loop, sc in next dc working **around** twisted Ch Loop) twice, ★ sc in next 20 dc, work Ch Loop, sc in next dc working **around** twisted Ch Loop, (sc in next 2 dc, work Ch Loop, sc in next dc working **around** twisted Ch Loop) twice; repeat from ★ across to last 15 dc, sc in last 15 dc.

Row 17: Ch 3, turn; keeping Ch Loops to **back** of work, dc in next sc and in each st across.

Row 18: Ch 1, turn; sc in first 19 dc, work Ch Loop, sc in next dc working **around** twisted Ch Loop, (sc in next 2 dc, work Ch Loop, sc in next dc working **around** twisted Ch Loop) twice, ★ sc in next 20 dc, work Ch Loop, sc in next dc working **around** twisted Ch Loop, (sc in next 2 dc, work Ch Loop, sc in next dc working **around** twisted Ch Loop) twice; repeat from ★ across to last 16 dc, sc in last 16 dc.

Row 19: Ch 3, turn; keeping Ch Loops to **back** of work, dc in next sc and in each st across.

Row 20: Ch 1, turn; sc in first 18 dc, work Ch Loop, sc in next dc working **around** twisted Ch Loop, (sc in next 2 dc, work Ch Loop, sc in next dc working **around** twisted Ch Loop) twice, ★ sc in next 20 dc, work Ch Loop, sc in next dc working **around** twisted Ch Loop, (sc in next 2 dc, work Ch Loop, sc in next dc working **around** twisted Ch Loop) twice; repeat from ★ across to last 17 dc, sc in last 17 dc.

Row 21: Ch 3, turn; keeping Ch Loops to **back** of work, dc in next sc and in each st across.

Row 22: Ch 1, turn; sc in first 17 dc, work Ch Loop, sc in next dc working **around** twisted Ch Loop, (sc in next 2 dc, work Ch Loop, sc in next dc working **around** twisted Ch Loop) twice, ★ sc in next 20 dc, work Ch Loop, sc in next dc working **around** twisted Ch Loop, (sc in next 2 dc, work Ch Loop, sc in next dc working **around** twisted Ch Loop) twice; repeat from ★ across to last 18 dc, sc in last 18 dc.

Row 23: Ch 3, turn; keeping Ch Loops to **back** of work, dc in next sc and in each st across.

Row 24: Ch 1, turn; sc in first 16 dc, work Ch Loop, sc in next dc working **around** twisted Ch Loop, (sc in next 2 dc, work Ch Loop, sc in next dc working **around** twisted Ch Loop) twice, ★ sc in next 20 dc, work Ch Loop, sc in next dc working **around** twisted Ch Loop, (sc in next 2 dc, work Ch Loop, sc in next dc working **around** twisted Ch Loop) twice; repeat from ★ across to last 19 dc, sc in last 19 dc.

Row 25: Ch 3, turn; keeping Ch Loops to **back** of work, dc in next sc and in each st across.

Row 26: Ch 1, turn; sc in first 15 dc, ★ work Ch Loop, sc in next dc working **around** twisted Ch Loop, (sc in next 2 dc, work Ch Loop, sc in next dc working **around** twisted Ch Loop) twice, sc in next 20 dc; repeat from ★ across.

Row 27: Ch 3, turn; keeping Ch Loops to **back** of work, dc in next sc and in each st across.

Rows 28-171: Repeat Rows 4-27, 6 times.

Row 172: Ch 1, turn; sc in first 15 dc, ★ sc in next dc working **around** twisted Ch Loop, (sc in next 3 dc, sc in next dc working **around** twisted Ch Loop) twice, sc in next 21 dc; repeat from ★ across; finish off.

Holding 4 strands of yarn together, each 18" long, add fringe between every two stitches across short edges of Afghan *(Figs. 27a & c, page 143)*.

COLORFUL COVERLET Continued from page 112.

ASSEMBLY

With Black, using Placement Diagram as a guide, and working through inside loops only, whipstitch Motifs together *(Fig. 26a, page 143)*, forming 13 horizontal strips, beginning in center ch of first corner ch-3 and ending in center ch of next corner ch-3; whipstitch strips together in same manner.

PLACEMENT DIAGRAM

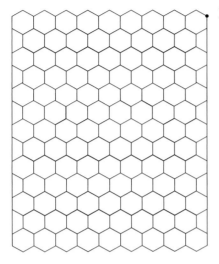 Point A

EDGING

With **right** side facing, join Black with slip st in corner ch-3 sp at Point A; ch 6, dc in same sp, † dc in next 9 sts, (dc, ch 3, dc) in next ch-3 sp, dc in next 9 sts, [decrease, dc in next 9 sts, (dc, ch 3, dc) in next ch-3 sp, dc in next 9 sts] 8 times, (dc, ch 3, dc) in next ch-3 sp, dc in next 9 sts, (dc in next ch, work 19 dc evenly spaced across next Half Motif, dc in next ch and in next 9 sts) 6 times †, (dc, ch 3, dc) in next ch-3 sp, repeat from † to † once; join with slip st to third ch of beginning ch-6, finish off.

Holding 14 strands of Black together, each 16" long, add fringe in points across short edges of Afghan *(Figs. 27a & c, page 143)*.

DUTCH ROSE Continued from page 114.

Rnd 4: Ch 3, 2 dc in same sp, dc in next dc, (dc in next ch-1 sp and in next dc) across to next corner ch-2 sp, ★ (3 dc, ch 2, 3 dc) in corner ch-2 sp, dc in next dc, (dc in next ch-1 sp and in next dc) across to next corner ch-2 sp; repeat from ★ 2 times **more**, 3 dc in same sp as first dc, ch 1, sc in first dc to form last ch-2 sp: 852 dc and 4 ch-2 sps.

Rnd 5: Ch 1, sc in same sp, ch 2, skip next dc, (sc in next dc, ch 2, skip next dc) across to next corner ch-2 sp, ★ sc in corner ch-2 sp, ch 2, skip next dc, (sc in next dc, ch 2, skip next dc) across to next corner ch-2 sp; repeat from ★ 2 times **more**; join with slip st to first sc, finish off.

PLACEMENT DIAGRAM

KEY

Square A

- Tan (Make 228)
- Red (Make 76)
- Green (Make 4)

Square B

- Tan & Red (Make 36)
- Tan & Green (Make 20)
- Tan & Lt Green (Make 4)
- Red & Lt Green (Make 8)
- Red & Green (Make 20)

DISTINCTIVE DESIGN

Splashes of green and burgundy are interwoven with gold to make this lively wrap! The distinctive design is created by long double crochets, and a striking green fringe completes the look.

Finished Size: 47$\frac{1}{2}$ " x 64$\frac{1}{2}$ "

MATERIALS
Worsted Weight Yarn:
Gold - 29$\frac{1}{2}$ ounces,
(840 grams, 2,025 yards)
Green - 17$\frac{1}{2}$ ounces,
(500 grams, 1,200 yards)
Burgundy - 15 ounces,
(430 grams, 1,030 yards)
Crochet hook, size H (5.00 mm) **or** size
needed for gauge

GAUGE: In pattern, 14 sts and
16 rows = 4"

Gauge Swatch: 4$\frac{1}{2}$ "w x 4"h
Ch 17 **loosely**.
Work same as Afghan for 16 rows.

STITCH GUIDE

LONG DOUBLE CROCHET (abbreviated LDC)
YO, working **around** previous row, insert hook in st or sp indicated, YO and pull up a loop even with last sc made, (YO and draw through 2 loops on hook) twice **(Fig. 9, page 140)**.

AFGHAN

With Green, ch 167 **loosely**.
Row 1 (Right side)**:** Sc in second ch from hook, ★ ch 2, skip next 2 chs, sc in next 4 chs; repeat from ★ across to last 3 chs, ch 2, skip next 2 chs, sc in last ch: 110 sc and 28 ch-2 sps.
Note: Loop a short piece of yarn around any stitch to mark Row 1 as **right** side.
Row 2: Ch 1, turn; sc in first sc, 2 sc in next ch-2 sp, (sc in next 4 sc, 2 sc in next ch-2 sp) across to last sc, sc in last sc; finish off: 166 sc.
Row 3: With **right** side facing, join Gold with sc in first sc **(see Joining With Sc, page 142)**; work 2 LDC in ch-2 sp one row **below** next 2 sc, sc in next sc, ★ ch 2, skip next 2 sc, sc in next sc, work 2 LDC in ch-2 sp one row **below** next 2 sc, sc in next sc; repeat from ★ across; do **not** finish off: 112 sts and 27 ch-2 sps.
Row 4: Ch 1, turn; sc in first 4 sts, (2 sc in next ch-2 sp, sc in next 4 sts) across; finish off: 166 sc.
Row 5: With **right** side facing, join Burgundy with sc in first sc; ch 2, skip next 2 sc, sc next sc, ★ work LDC in each of 2 skipped sc 2 rows **below** next 2 sc, sc in next sc, ch 2, skip next 2 sc, sc in next sc; repeat from ★ across; do **not** finish off: 110 sts and 28 ch-2 sps.
Row 6: Ch 1, turn; sc in first sc, 2 sc in next ch-2 sp, (sc in next 4 sts, 2 sc in next ch-2 sp) across to last sc, sc in last sc; finish off: 166 sc.
Row 7: With **right** side facing, join Gold with sc in first sc; work LDC in each of 2 skipped sc 2 rows **below** next 2 sc, sc in next sc, ★ ch 2, skip next 2 sc, sc in next sc, work LDC in each of 2 skipped sc 2 rows **below** next 2 sc, sc in next sc; repeat from ★ across; do **not** finish off: 112 sts and 27 ch-2 sps.
Row 8: Ch 1, turn; sc in first 4 sts, (2 sc in next ch-2 sp, sc in next 4 sts) across; finish off: 166 sc.
Rows 9 and 10: With Green, repeat Rows 5 and 6.
Rows 11 and 12: Repeat Rows 7 and 8.

Repeat Rows 5-12 until Afghan measures approximately 64" from beginning ch, ending by working Row 8.

Next Row: With **right** side facing, join Green with sc in first sc; sc in next 3 sc, ★ work LDC in each of 2 skipped sc 2 rows **below** next 2 sc, sc in next 4 sc; repeat from ★ across; do **not** finish off.

Last Row: Ch 1, turn; sc in first sc, ★ ch 2, skip next 2 sc, sc in next 4 sts; repeat from ★ across to last 3 sc, ch 2, skip next 2 sc, sc in last sc; finish off.

Holding 8 strands of Green together, each 22" long, add fringe in sps across short edges of Afghan *(Figs. 27a & c, page 143)*.

WINTER WHITE

*When the cold weather keeps you indoors, grab a book and a hot
drink and curl up with this winter warmer! A circle of clusters punctuates
each of the crocheted squares, creating an illusion of snowy pinwheels.*

Finished Size: 47" x 67"

MATERIALS
Worsted Weight Yarn:
    50 ounces, (1,420 grams, 3,285 yards)
Crochet hook, size H (5.00 mm) **or** size needed
    for gauge
Yarn needle

GAUGE SWATCH: 4"
Work same as Square.

STITCH GUIDE

> **FRONT POST TREBLE CROCHET** *(abbreviated FPtr)*
> YO twice, insert hook from **front** to **back** around post of st
> indicated, YO and pull up a loop *(Fig. 12, page 141)*,
> (YO and draw through 2 loops on hook) 3 times.
>
> **CLUSTER**
> Ch 3, YO, insert hook in third ch from hook, YO and pull up
> a loop, YO and draw through 2 loops on hook, YO, insert
> hook in **same** ch, YO and pull up a loop, YO and draw
> through 2 loops on hook, YO and draw through all 3 loops
> on hook *(Figs. 15a & b, page 141)*.

SQUARE (Make 176)
Rnd 1 (Right side): Ch 5, (dc, ch 1) 7 times in fifth ch from
hook; join with slip st to fourth ch of beginning ch-5: 8 ch-1 sps.
Note: Loop a short piece of yarn around any stitch to mark
Rnd 1 as **right** side.
Rnd 2: Slip st in first ch-1 sp, ch 3 **(counts as first dc)**, dc in
same sp, work FPtr around next dc, (2 dc in next ch-1 sp, work
FPtr around next st) around; join with slip st to first dc: 24 sts.
Rnd 3: Ch 1, **turn**; sc in same st, work Cluster, skip next FPtr,
★ sc in next st, work Cluster, skip next st; repeat from ★
around; join with slip st to first sc: 12 Clusters.
Rnd 4: Ch 3, do **not** turn; working in **front** of Clusters, dc in
next skipped FPtr on Rnd 2, ch 1, ★ hdc in next sc on Rnd 3,
ch 1, dc in next skipped st on Rnd 2, ch 1; repeat from ★
around; join with slip st to second ch of beginning ch-3: 24 sts
and 24 ch-1 sps.

Rnd 5: Ch 1, **turn**; sc in same st, ch 1, hdc in next dc, ch 1,
(dc, ch 3, dc) in next hdc, ch 1, hdc in next dc, ch 1, sc in next
hdc, ch 1, slip st in next dc, ch 1, ★ sc in next hdc, ch 1, hdc in
next dc, ch 1, (dc, ch 3, dc) in next hdc, ch 1, hdc in next dc,
ch 1, sc in next hdc, ch 1, slip st in next dc, ch 1; repeat from ★
2 times **more**; join with slip st to first sc, finish off: 28 sts and
28 sps.

ASSEMBLY
Working through both loops, whipstitch Squares together
(Fig. 26b, page 143), forming 11 vertical strips of
16 Squares each, beginning in center ch of first corner ch-3 and
ending in center ch of next corner ch-3; whipstitch strips
together in same manner.

EDGING
Rnd 1: With **right** side facing, join yarn with sc in any corner
ch-3 sp *(see Joining With Sc, page 142)*; ch 3, sc in same
sp, ch 1, (sc in next sp, ch 1) across to next corner ch-3 sp,
★ (sc, ch 3, sc) in corner ch-3 sp, ch 1, (sc in next sp, ch 1)
across to next corner ch-3 sp; repeat from ★ 2 times **more**;
join with slip st to first sc: 432 sc and 4 ch-3 sps.
Rnd 2: Ch 4, (dc, ch 3, dc) in next corner ch-3 sp, ch 1, ★ (dc
in next sc, ch 1) across to next corner ch-3 sp, (dc, ch 3, dc) in
corner ch-3 sp, ch 1; repeat from ★ 2 times **more**, (dc in next
sc, ch 1) across; join with slip st to third ch of beginning ch-4:
436 ch-1 sps and 4 ch-3 sps.
Rnd 3: Slip st in first ch-1 sp, ch 1, **turn**; sc in same sp, (work
Cluster, skip next ch-1 sp, sc in next ch-1 sp) across to next
corner ch-3 sp, work (Cluster, sc, Cluster) in corner ch-3 sp,
★ sc in next ch-1 sp, (work Cluster, skip next ch-1 sp, sc in
next ch-1 sp) across to next corner ch-3 sp, work (Cluster, sc,
Cluster) in corner ch-3 sp; repeat from ★ 2 times **more**; join
with slip st to first sc: 224 Clusters.

Rnd 4: Ch 1, turn; sc in same st, ch 1, working in sps **behind** Clusters and in sc on Rnd 3, dc in ch-3 sp **below** next Cluster, ch 1, (hdc, ch 3, hdc) in next corner sc, ch 1, dc in same sp **below** next Cluster, ch 1, ★ (sc in next sc, ch 1, dc in sp **below** next Cluster, ch 1) across to next corner sc, (hdc, ch 3, hdc) in corner sc, ch 1, dc in same sp **below** next Cluster, ch 1; repeat from ★ 2 times **more**, (sc in next sc, ch 1, dc in ch-1 sp **below** next Cluster, ch 1) across; join with slip st to first sc.

Rnd 5: Slip st in first ch-1 sp, ch 1, do **not** turn; slip st in next ch-1 sp, ch 1, (slip st, ch 2, slip st) in next corner ch-3 sp, ch 1, ★ (slip st in next ch-1 sp, ch 1) across to next corner ch-3 sp, (slip st, ch 2, slip st) in corner ch-3 sp, ch 1; repeat from ★ 2 times **more**, (slip st in next ch-1 sp, ch 1) across; join with slip st to first slip st, finish off.

SOOTHING RIPPLES

Ripples in soothing tones soften this formal throw. Textured cluster stitches dot the ripples, which run across the width of the throw and create a novel side fringe.

Finished Size: 52" x 70"

MATERIALS

Worsted Weight Yarn:

Black - 35 ounces, (990 grams, 1,980 yards)
Rose - 12 ounces, (340 grams, 680 yards)
Lt Teal - 11 ounces, (310 grams, 620 yards)
Pink - 6 ounces, (170 grams, 340 yards)
Teal - 5¹/₂ ounces, (160 grams, 310 yards)
Crochet hook, size I (5.50 mm) **or** size needed for gauge

GAUGE: Each repeat, from point to point = 3¹/₄";
6 rows = 3"

Gauge Swatch: 9³/₄"w x 3"h
Ch 49 **loosely**.
Work same as Afghan Body for 6 rows.

When joining yarn and finishing off, always leave a 7" end to be worked into fringe.

STITCH GUIDE

DECREASE (uses next 3 sts)
YO, † insert hook in **next** st, YO and pull up a loop, YO and draw through 2 loops on hook †, YO, skip next st, repeat from † to † once, YO and draw through all 3 loops on hook **(counts as one dc).**
CLUSTER (uses one st)
★ YO twice, insert hook in st indicated, YO and pull up a loop, (YO and draw through 2 loops on hook) twice; repeat from ★ 3 times **more**, YO and draw through all 5 loops on hook **(Figs. 15a & b, page 141).**

COLOR SEQUENCE

One row **each**: Black, Rose, Black, Pink, Black, Rose, Black, ★ Lt Teal, Black, Teal, Black, Lt Teal, Black, Rose, Black, Pink, Black, Rose, Black; repeat from ★ throughout.

AFGHAN BODY

With Black, ch 244 **loosely**, place marker in third ch from hook for st placement.

Row 1 (Right side)**:** Dc in fifth ch from hook **(4 skipped chs count as first dc plus one skipped ch)**, ch 1, (skip next ch, dc in next ch, ch 1) twice, skip next ch, (dc, ch 3, dc) in next ch, ch 1, (skip next ch, dc in next ch, ch 1) twice, ★ skip next ch, YO, insert hook in next ch, YO and pull up a loop, YO and draw through 2 loops on hook, YO, skip next 2 chs, insert hook in next ch, YO and pull up a loop, YO and draw through 2 loops on hook, YO and draw through all 3 loops on hook, ch 1, (skip next ch, dc in next ch, ch 1) twice, skip next ch, (dc, ch 3, dc) in next ch, ch 1, (skip next ch, dc in next ch, ch 1) twice; repeat from ★ across to last 4 chs, skip next ch, decrease; finish off: 112 sps.

Note: Loop a short piece of yarn around any stitch to mark Row 1 as **right** side.

Row 2: With **wrong** side facing, join Rose with sc in first dc **(see Joining With Sc, page 142)**; (ch 1, sc in next dc) 3 times, (sc, ch 2, sc) in next ch-3 sp, sc in next dc, (ch 1, sc in next dc) twice, ★ skip next ch-1 sp, work Cluster in next st, sc in next dc, (ch 1, sc in next dc) twice, (sc, ch 2, sc) in next ch-3 sp, sc in next dc, (ch 1, sc in next dc) twice; repeat from ★ across to last 2 dc, ch 1, skip next dc, sc in last dc; finish off: 130 sc and 15 Clusters.

Row 3: With **right** side facing, join Black with slip st in first sc; ch 3, dc in next sc, ★ ch 1, (dc in next sc, ch 1) twice, (dc, ch 3, dc) in next ch-2 sp, ch 1, skip next sc, (dc in next sc, ch 1) twice, skip next ch, decrease; repeat from ★ across; finish off: 113 dc.

Row 4: With **wrong** side facing, join next color with sc in first dc; (ch 1, sc in next dc) 3 times, (sc, ch 2, sc) in next ch-3 sp, sc in next dc, (ch 1, sc in next dc) twice, ★ work Cluster in next dc, sc in next dc, (ch 1, sc in next dc) twice, (sc, ch 2, sc) in next ch-3 sp, sc in next dc, (ch 1, sc in next dc) twice; repeat from ★ across to last dc, ch 1, skip last dc, sc in next ch; finish off.

Rows 5-139: Repeat Rows 3 and 4, 67 times; then repeat Row 3 once **more.**

EDGING
TOP

With **right** side facing and working in sts on Row 139, join Black with slip st in top of beginning ch-3; (slip st in next ch-1 sp, ch 1) 3 times, (slip st, ch 2, slip st) in next ch-3 sp, ch 1, ★ (slip st in next ch-1 sp, ch 1) 6 times, (slip st, ch 2, slip st) in next ch-3 sp, ch 1; repeat from ★ across to last 3 ch-1 sps, (slip st in next ch-1 sp, ch 1) twice, slip st in last ch-1 sp and in last dc; finish off.

BOTTOM

With **right** side facing and working in sps and in free loops of beginning ch (*Fig. 21b, page 142*), join Black with slip st in first ch; (slip st in next ch-1 sp, ch 1) 7 times, ★ (slip st, ch 2, slip st) in next ch-2 sp, ch 1, (slip st in next ch-1 sp, ch 1) 6 times; repeat from ★ across to last sp, slip st in last sp and in marked ch; finish off.

Holding 3 strands **each** of Black and corresponding color together, each 14" long, add additional fringe in each wrong side row across long edges of Afghan (*Figs. 27b & d, page 143*).

COUNTRY WARMER

This country throw is teeming with rich colors to banish the winter blahs! It's worked in squares that are fashioned to create a decorative pattern of zigzagging strips. Plush popcorns add a wealth of texture to the spectacular spread.

Finished Size: 55" x 72½"

MATERIALS
Worsted Weight Yarn:
Purple - 29 ounces, (820 grams, 1,640 yards)
Brown - 28 ounces, (800 grams, 1,585 yards)
Rose - 26 ounces, (740 grams, 1,470 yards)
Teal - 23 ounces, (650 grams, 1,300 yards)
Crochet hook, size F (3.75 mm) **or** size needed
for gauge
Yarn needle

GAUGE: Each Square = 8¾"

Gauge Swatch: 8¾"w x 2¼"h
Work same as Square through Row 6.

STITCH GUIDE

LONG SINGLE CROCHET (abbreviated LSC)
Working **around** last 3 dc made, insert hook in skipped sc, YO and pull up a loop even with last st made, YO and draw through both loops on hook **(Fig. 9, page 140)**.
RIB
★ YO, insert hook from **front** to **back** around post of st indicated **(Fig. 10, page 140)**, YO and pull up a loop; repeat from ★ once **more**, YO and draw through all 5 loops on hook.
POPCORN
3 Dc in sc indicated, drop loop from hook, insert hook in first dc of 3-dc group, hook dropped loop and draw through, ch 1 to close.

SQUARE (Make 48)
With Teal, ch 35 **loosely**.
Row 1 (Right side)**:** Sc in back ridge of second ch from hook and each ch across **(Fig. 2b, page 139)**: 34 sc.
Note: Loop a short piece of yarn around any stitch to mark Row 1 as **right** side and bottom edge.
Row 2: Ch 3 **(counts as first dc, now and throughout)**, turn; ★ skip next sc, dc in next 3 sc, work LSC; repeat from ★ across to last sc, dc in last sc: 8 LSC.

Row 3: Ch 1, turn; sc in each st across: 34 sc.
Row 4: Ch 3, turn; ★ skip next sc, dc in next 3 sc, work LSC; repeat from ★ across to last sc, dc in last sc.
Rows 5 and 6: Repeat Rows 3 and 4.
Finish off.
Row 7: With **wrong** side facing, join Purple with sc in first dc **(see Joining With Sc, page 142)**; sc in next dc and in each st across: 34 sc.
Row 8: Ch 1, turn; sc in first 3 sc, work Rib around next sc, (sc in next 2 sc, work Rib around next sc) across to last 3 sc, sc in last 3 sc: 10 Ribs.
Row 9: Ch 1, turn; sc in each st across: 34 sc.
Row 10: Ch 1, turn; sc in first 3 sc, work Rib around Rib one row **below** next sc, (sc in next 2 sc, work Rib around Rib one row **below** next sc) across to last 3 sc, sc in last 3 sc: 10 Ribs.
Rows 11-16: Repeat Rows 9 and 10, 3 times.
Finish off.
Row 17: With **wrong** side facing, join Rose with sc in first sc; dc in next sc, (sc in next st, dc in next st) across: 34 sts.
Rows 18-24: Ch 1, turn; sc in first dc, dc in next sc, (sc in next dc, dc in next sc) across.
Finish off.
Row 25: With **wrong** side facing, join Brown with sc in first dc; sc in next sc and in each st across.
Row 26: Ch 1, turn; sc in first 2 sc, (work Popcorn in next sc, sc in next 3 sc) across: 8 Popcorns.
Row 27: Ch 1, turn; sc in each st across: 34 sc.
Row 28: Ch 1, turn; sc in first 4 sc, work Popcorn in next sc, (sc in next 3 sc, work Popcorn in next sc) across to last 5 sc, sc in last 5 sc: 7 Popcorns.
Row 29: Ch 1, turn; sc in each st across: 34 sc.
Rows 30-33: Repeat Rows 26-29.
Finish off.

ASSEMBLY
With desired color, using photo as a guide, alternating bottom of Squares, and working through **both** loops of sts and in end of rows, sew Squares together forming 6 vertical strips of 8 Squares each **(Fig. 25, page 143)**; sew strips together.

EDGING

Rnd 1: With **right** side facing, join Teal with sc in any corner; sc in same st, working in sts and across end of rows, ★ † work 33 sc evenly spaced across first Square, work 34 sc evenly spaced across each Square across †, 3 sc in corner; repeat from ★ 2 times **more**, then repeat from † to † once, sc in same st as first sc; join with slip st to first sc: 960 sc.

Rnd 2: Ch 1, (sc, ch 1) twice in same st, ★ † skip next sc, (sc in next sc, ch 1, skip next sc) across to center sc of next corner 3-sc group †, (sc, ch 1) twice in center sc; repeat from ★ 2 times **more**, then repeat from † to † once; join with slip st to first sc, finish off.

Rnd 3: With **right** side facing, join Purple with sc in any corner ch-1 sp; ch 1, sc in same sp, ch 1, (sc in next ch-1 sp, ch 1) across to next corner ch-1 sp, ★ (sc, ch 1) twice in corner ch-1 sp, (sc in next ch-1 sp, ch 1) across to next corner ch-1 sp; repeat from ★ 2 times **more**; join with slip st to first sc.

Rnd 4: Slip st in first corner ch-1 sp, ch 1, (sc in same sp, ch 1) twice, (sc in next ch-1 sp, ch 1) across to next corner ch-1 sp, ★ (sc, ch 1) twice in corner ch-1 sp, (sc in next ch-1 sp, ch 1) across to next corner ch-1 sp; repeat from ★ 2 times **more**; join with slip st to first sc, finish off.

Rnds 5 and 6: With Rose, repeat Rnds 3 and 4.

SANTA'S SPREAD

Be careful where you drape this festive throw — it could entice even Santa to sit back and relax for a spell! Traditional Yuletide colors make it a perfect holiday accent. Long double crochets create a dangling "icicle" effect.

december

Finished Size: 49" x 67"

MATERIALS
Worsted Weight Yarn:
Natural - 30 ounces,
(850 grams, 2,065 yards)
Green - 13½ ounces,
(380 grams, 930 yards)
Burgundy - 13½ ounces,
(380 grams, 930 yards)
Crochet hook, size H (5.00 mm) **or** size needed for gauge

GAUGE: In pattern, 14 sts and 12 rows = 4";
4 repeats (16 sts) = 4½"

Gauge Swatch: 4¼" square
Ch 16 **loosely**.
Work same as Afghan for 13 rows.

STITCH GUIDE

> **LONG DOUBLE CROCHET (abbreviated LDC)**
> YO, working **around** previous row, insert hook in ch-1 sp one row **below** next ch, YO and pull up a loop even with last sc made, (YO and draw through 2 loops on hook) twice **(Fig. 9, page 140)**.

AFGHAN

With Natural, ch 172 **loosely**.
Row 1 (Wrong side)**:** Sc in second ch from hook and in each ch across; finish off: 171 sc.
Note: Loop a short piece of yarn around **back** of any stitch to mark **right** side.
Row 2: With **right** side facing, join Green with slip st in first sc; ch 4 **(counts as first dc plus ch 1, now and throughout)**, skip next sc, dc in next 3 sc, ★ ch 1, skip next sc, dc in next 3 sc; repeat from ★ across to last 2 sc, ch 1, skip next sc, dc in last sc; do **not** finish off: 128 dc and 43 ch-1 sps.
Row 3: Ch 1, turn; sc in first dc, ch 1, (sc in next 3 dc, ch 1) across to last dc, sc in last dc; finish off.
Row 4: With **right** side facing, join Natural with sc in first sc **(see Joining With Sc, page 142)**; work LDC, (sc in next 3 sc, work LDC) across to last sc, sc in last sc; do **not** finish off: 171 sts.
Row 5: Ch 1, turn; sc in each st across; finish off.
Row 6: With **right** side facing, join Burgundy with slip st in first sc; ch 4, skip next sc, dc in next 3 sc, ★ ch 1, skip next sc, dc in next 3 sc; repeat from ★ across to last 2 sc, ch 1, skip next sc, dc in last sc; do **not** finish off: 128 dc and 43 ch-1 sps.
Row 7: Ch 1, turn; sc in first dc, ch 1, (sc in next 3 dc, ch 1) across to last dc, sc in last dc; finish off.
Row 8: With **right** side facing, join Natural with sc in first sc; work LDC, (sc in next 3 sc, work LDC) across to last sc, sc in last sc; do **not** finish off: 171 sts.
Row 9: Ch 1, turn; sc in each st across; finish off.
Repeat Rows 2-9 until Afghan measures approximately 66½" from beginning ch, ending by working Row 7.

Continued on page 137.

EMERALD TREASURE

*Add warmth to his private retreat by stationing this handsome
throw in his favorite easy chair. Fashioned in simple-to-make strips,
the "comforting" companion looks dynamic in deep emerald green.*

Finished Size: 44" x 58"

MATERIALS
Worsted Weight Yarn:
  35½ ounces, (1,010 grams, 1,925 yards)
Crochet hook, size G (4.00 mm) **or** size needed
  for gauge

GAUGE: Each Strip = 5½ " wide

Gauge Swatch: 5½ "w x 6¾ "h
Work same as Center through Row 10; do **not** finish off.
Work First Side Edging.
Work Second Side Edging.

FIRST STRIP
CENTER
Ch 7 **loosely**.

Row 1 (Right side): 2 Dc in sixth ch from hook, ch 2, 2 dc in
last ch: one ch-2 sp.

Note: Loop a short piece of yarn around any stitch to mark
Row 1 as **right** side and bottom edge.

Rows 2-86: Ch 5, turn; (2 dc, ch 2, 2 dc) in ch-2 sp; do **not**
finish off.

FIRST SIDE EDGING
Row 1: Ch 7 (**counts as first dc plus ch 4, now and
throughout**), do **not** turn; working in ch-5 sps at end of rows,
(sc in next ch-5 sp, ch 4) across to last ch-5 sp, sc in center ch
of last ch-5: 43 ch-4 sps.

Row 2: Ch 1, turn; sc in first sc, 4 sc in next ch-4 sp, sc in next
sc, (5 sc in next ch-4 sp, sc in next sc) across to last ch-4 sp,
4 sc in last ch-4 sp, sc in last dc: 257 sc.

Row 3: Ch 4 (**counts as first dc plus ch 1**), turn; skip next
sc, dc in next sc, ★ ch 1, skip next sc, dc in next sc; repeat from
★ across: 129 dc and 128 ch-1 sps.

Row 4: Ch 1, turn; sc in each dc and in each ch-1 sp across:
257 sc.

Row 5: Ch 1, turn; sc in first sc, ★ ch 5, skip next 3 sc, sc in
next sc; repeat from ★ across; finish off: 64 ch-5 sps.

SECOND SIDE EDGING
Row 1: With **wrong** side facing, join yarn with slip st in free
loop of first ch of beginning ch-7 *(Fig. 21b, page 142)*; ch 7,
(sc in next ch-5 sp, ch 4) across to last ch-5 sp, sc in center ch
of last ch-5: 43 ch-4 sps.

Rows 2-5: Work same as First Side Edging.

REMAINING 7 STRIPS
Work same as First Strip through Row 4 of Second Side Edging.

Row 5 (Joining row): Ch 1, turn; sc in first sc, ch 2, holding
Strips with **right** sides together and bottom edges at same end,
sc in first ch-5 sp on **previous Strip**, ch 2, skip next 3 sc on
new Strip, sc in next sc, ★ ch 2, sc in next ch-5 sp on
previous Strip, ch 2, skip next 3 sc on **new Strip**, sc in next
sc; repeat from ★ across; finish off.

Holding 8 strands of yarn together, each 16" long, add fringe
evenly spaced across short edges of Afghan *(Figs. 27b & d,
page 143)*.

RUBY LACE

Wrap up your holidays by adding this regal comforter to your gift list. Fashioned in a rich ruby red, the lacy comforter features a pattern of openwork fans created with three simple stitches. It's so easy to make, you might be tempted to crochet two!

Finished Size: 46" x 60"

MATERIALS

Worsted Weight Yarn:
31½ ounces, (890 grams, 2,160 yards)
Crochet hook, size H (5.00 mm) **or** size needed
for gauge

GAUGE: In pattern, one repeat = 4¼"; 10 rows = 4½"

Gauge Swatch: 6½"w x 4½"h
Ch 29 **loosely**.
Work same as Afghan Body for 10 rows.
Finish off.

AFGHAN BODY

Ch 173 **loosely**, place marker in fifth ch from hook for
st placement.
Row 1 (Right side): Sc in seventh ch from hook, ★ ch 5, skip
next 3 chs, sc in next ch; repeat from ★ across to last 2 chs,
ch 2, skip next ch, dc in last ch: 43 sps.
Note: Loop a short piece of yarn around any stitch to mark
Row 1 as **right** side.
Row 2: Ch 1, turn; sc in first ch-2 sp, ★ (ch 5, sc in next
ch-5 sp) twice, 8 dc in next ch-5 sp, sc in next ch-5 sp; repeat
from ★ across to last 2 sps, (ch 5, sc in next sp) twice: 80 dc
and 22 ch-5 sps.
Row 3: Ch 5, turn; sc in first ch-5 sp, ch 5, sc in next ch-5 sp,
★ ch 4, skip next dc, dc in next 6 dc, ch 4, sc in next ch-5 sp,
ch 5, sc in next ch-5 sp; repeat from ★ across to last sc, ch 2,
dc in last sc: 60 dc and 33 sps.
Row 4: Ch 1, turn; sc in first ch-2 sp, (ch 5, sc in next sp)
twice, ★ ch 3, skip next dc, dc in next 4 dc, ch 3, sc in next
ch-4 sp, (ch 5, sc in next sp) twice; repeat from ★ across: 40 dc
and 42 sps.

Row 5: Ch 5, turn; sc in first ch-5 sp, ch 5, sc in next ch-5 sp,
★ ch 5, sc in next ch-3 sp, ch 3, skip next dc, dc in next 2 dc,
ch 3, sc in next ch-3 sp, (ch 5, sc in next ch-5 sp) twice; repeat
from ★ across to last sc, ch 2, dc in last sc: 20 dc and 53 sps.
Row 6: Ch 1, turn; sc in first ch-2 sp, 8 dc in next ch-5 sp, sc in
next ch-5 sp, ★ ch 5, skip next dc, sc in sp **before** next dc,
ch 5, skip next ch-3 sp, sc in next ch-5 sp, 8 dc in next ch-5 sp,
sc in next ch-5 sp; repeat from ★ across: 88 dc and 20 ch-5 sps.
Row 7: Ch 4, turn; skip next dc, dc in next 6 dc, ★ ch 4, sc in
next ch-5 sp, ch 5, sc in next ch-5 sp, ch 4, skip next dc, dc in
next 6 dc; repeat from ★ across to last 2 sts, ch 1, skip next dc,
dc in last sc: 66 dc and 32 sps.
Row 8: Ch 5, turn; sc in first ch-1 sp, ch 3, skip next dc, dc in
next 4 dc, ch 3, ★ sc in next ch-4 sp, (ch 5, sc in next ch-5 sp)
twice, ch 3, skip next dc, dc in next 4 dc, ch 3; repeat from ★
across to last ch-4 sp, (sc, ch 2, dc) in last ch-4 sp: 44 dc and
44 sps.
Row 9: Ch 5, turn; skip first ch-2 sp, sc in next ch-3 sp, ch 3,
skip next dc, dc in next 2 dc, ch 3, sc in next ch-3 sp, ★ ch 5,
(sc in next ch-5 sp, ch 5) twice, sc in next ch-3 sp, ch 3, skip
next dc, dc in next 2 dc, ch 3, sc in next ch-3 sp; repeat from ★
across to last ch-5 sp, ch 2, dc in last ch-5 sp: 22 dc and 54 sps.
Row 10: Ch 1, turn; sc in first ch-2 sp, ch 5, skip next dc, sc in
sp **before** next dc, ch 5, ★ skip next ch-3 sp, sc in next ch-5 sp,
8 dc in next ch-5 sp, sc in next ch-5 sp, ch 5, skip next dc, sc in
sp **before** next dc, ch 5; repeat from ★ across to last 2 sps, skip
next ch-3 sp, sc in last ch-5 sp: 80 dc and 22 ch-5 sps.
Rows 11-129: Repeat Rows 3-10, 14 times; then repeat
Rows 3-9 once **more**.
Row 130: Ch 1, turn; sc in first ch-2 sp, ch 3, sc in next 2 dc,
★ ch 3, skip next ch-3 sp, (sc in next ch-5 sp, ch 3) 3 times, sc
in next 2 dc; repeat from ★ across to last 2 sps, ch 3, skip next
ch-3 sp, sc in last ch-5 sp; do **not** finish off.

Continued on page 137.

132

APPEALING ARAN

Simply beautiful, this Aran afghan is distinguished by alternating panels of diamonds and popcorns. The rugged style will add a wealth of character to any setting.

Finished Size: 49" x 69½"

MATERIALS
Worsted Weight Yarn:
64 ounces, (1,820 grams, 3,620 yards)
Crochet hook, size I (5.50 mm) **or** size needed
for gauge
Yarn needle

GAUGE: In pattern, 7 rows = 4¼"
Panel A = 2¾" wide
Panel B = 4¾" wide

Gauge Swatch: 2¾" w x 4¼" h
Work same as Panel A through Row 7.

STITCH GUIDE

BACK POST TREBLE CROCHET *(abbreviated BPtr)*
YO twice, insert hook from **back** to **front** around post of st indicated *(Fig. 14, page 141)*, YO and pull up a loop, (YO and draw through 2 loops on hook) 3 times.

FRONT POST TREBLE CROCHET *(abbreviated FPtr)*
YO twice, insert hook from **front** to **back** around post of st indicated *(Fig. 12, page 141)*, YO and pull up a loop, (YO and draw through 2 loops on hook) 3 times.

CABLE
Ch 5 **loosely**, slip st from **front** to **back** around post of dc 2 rows **below** last dc made *(Fig. 1a)*, hdc in top loop of each ch just made *(Fig. 1b)*.

Fig. 1a

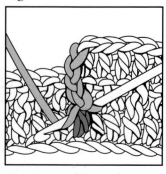

Fig. 1b

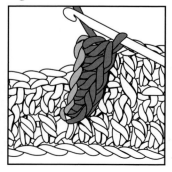

POPCORN
5 Dc in dc indicated, drop loop from hook, insert hook in first dc of 5-dc group, hook dropped loop and draw through *(Fig. 17, page 141)*.

PANEL A (Make 7)
Ch 11 **loosely**.
Row 1 (Right side): Dc in fourth ch from hook **(3 skipped chs count as first dc, now and throughout)** and in each ch across: 9 dc.
Note: Loop a short piece of yarn around any stitch to mark Row 1 as **right** side and bottom edge.
Row 2: Ch 3 **(counts as first dc, now and throughout)**, turn; work BPtr around next dc, dc in next 5 dc, work BPtr around next dc, dc in last dc.
Row 3: Ch 3, turn; work FPtr around next BPtr, dc in next 3 dc, work Cable, dc in next 2 dc, work FPtr around next BPtr, dc in last dc.
Row 4: Ch 3, turn; work BPtr around next FPtr, dc in next 5 dc, work BPtr around next FPtr, dc in last dc.
Row 5: Ch 3, turn; work FPtr around next BPtr, dc in next 3 dc, working to **right** of previous Cable *(Fig. 2)*, work Cable, dc in next 2 dc, work FPtr around next BPtr, dc in last dc.

Fig. 2

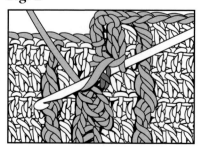

Rows 6-8: Repeat Rows 4 and 5 once, then repeat Row 4 once **more**.
Row 9: Ch 3, turn; work FPtr around next BPtr, dc in next 5 dc, work FPtr around next BPtr, dc in last dc; do **not** finish off.

Continued on page 136.

Row 10: Ch 3, turn; work BPtr around next FPtr, dc in next 5 dc, work BPtr around next FPtr, dc in last dc.

Row 11: Ch 3, turn; work FPtr around next BPtr, dc in next 2 dc, work Popcorn in next dc, dc in next 2 dc, work FPtr around next BPtr, dc in last dc.

Row 12: Ch 3, turn; work BPtr around next FPtr, dc in next 5 sts, work BPtr around next FPtr, dc in last dc.

Rows 13-16: Repeat Rows 11 and 12 twice.

Row 17: Ch 3, turn; work FPtr around next BPtr, dc in next 5 dc, work FPtr around next BPtr, dc in last dc.

Row 18: Ch 3, turn; work BPtr around next FPtr, dc in next 5 dc, work BPtr around next FPtr, dc in last dc.

Rows 19-113: Repeat Rows 3-18, 5 times, then repeat Rows 3-17 once **more**.
Finish off.

PANEL B (Make 6)

Ch 18 **loosely**.

Row 1: Dc in fourth ch from hook and in each ch across: 16 dc.

Row 2 (Right side): Ch 3, turn; work FPtr around next dc, dc in next 4 dc, work FPtr around each of next 4 dc, dc in next 4 dc, work FPtr around next dc, dc in last dc.

Note: Mark Row 2 as **right** side and bottom edge.

Row 3: Ch 3, turn; work BPtr around next FPtr, dc in next 3 dc, skip next dc, work BPtr around each of next 2 FPtr, dc in same FPtr just worked around and in next FPtr, work BPtr around same FPtr just worked into and around next FPtr, skip next dc, dc in next 3 dc, work BPtr around next FPtr, dc in last dc.

Row 4: Ch 3, turn; work FPtr around next BPtr, dc in next 2 dc, skip next dc, work FPtr around each of next 2 BPtr, dc in same BPtr just worked around and in next 3 sts, work FPtr around same BPtr just worked into and around next BPtr, skip next dc, dc in next 2 dc, work FPtr around next BPtr, dc in last dc.

Row 5: Ch 3, turn; work BPtr around next FPtr, dc in next dc, skip next dc, work BPtr around each of next 2 FPtr, dc in same FPtr just worked around and in next 5 sts, work BPtr around same FPtr just worked into and around next FPtr, skip next dc, dc in next dc, work BPtr around next FPtr, dc in last dc.

Row 6: Ch 3, turn; work FPtr around next BPtr, dc in next 2 sts, work FPtr around same BPtr just worked into and around next BPtr, skip next dc, dc in next 4 dc, skip next dc, work FPtr around each of next 2 BPtr, dc in same BPtr just worked around and in next dc, work FPtr around next BPtr, dc in last dc.

Row 7: Ch 3, turn; work BPtr around next FPtr, dc in next 3 sts, work BPtr around same FPtr just worked into and around next FPtr, skip next dc, dc in next 2 dc, skip next dc, work BPtr around each of next 2 FPtr, dc in same FPtr just worked around and in next 2 dc, work BPtr around next FPtr, dc in last dc.

Row 8: Ch 3, turn; work FPtr around next BPtr, dc in next 4 sts, work FPtr around same BPtr just worked into and around next BPtr, skip next 2 dc, work FPtr around each of next 2 BPtr, dc in same BPtr just worked around and in next 3 dc, work FPtr around next BPtr, dc in last dc.

Row 9: Ch 3, turn; work BPtr around next FPtr, dc in next 4 dc, skip next 2 FPtr, work BPtr around each of next 2 FPtr, working **behind** 2 BPtr just made, work BPtr around first skipped FPtr and around next FPtr, dc in next 4 dc, work BPtr around next FPtr, dc in last dc.

Row 10: Ch 3, turn; work FPtr around next BPtr, dc in next 3 dc, skip next dc, work FPtr around each of next 2 BPtr, dc in same BPtr just worked around and in next BPtr, work FPtr around same BPtr just worked into and around next BPtr, skip next dc, dc in next 3 dc, work FPtr around next BPtr, dc in last dc.

Row 11: Ch 3, turn; work BPtr around next FPtr, dc in next 2 dc, skip next dc, work BPtr around each of next 2 FPtr, dc in same FPtr just worked around and in next 3 sts, work BPtr around same FPtr just worked into and around next FPtr, skip next dc, dc in next 2 dc, work BPtr around next FPtr, dc in last dc.

Row 12: Ch 3, turn; work FPtr around next BPtr, dc in next dc, skip next dc, work FPtr around each of next 2 BPtr, dc in same BPtr just worked around and in next 5 sts, work FPtr around same BPtr just worked into and around next BPtr, skip next dc, dc in next dc, work FPtr around next BPtr, dc in last dc.

Row 13: Ch 3, turn; work BPtr around next FPtr, dc in next 2 sts, work BPtr around same FPtr just worked into and around next FPtr, skip next dc, dc in next 4 dc, skip next dc, work BPtr around each of next 2 FPtr, dc in same FPtr just worked around and in next dc, work BPtr around next FPtr, dc in last dc.

Row 14: Ch 3, turn; work FPtr around next BPtr, dc in next 3 sts, work FPtr around same BPtr just worked into and around next BPtr, skip next dc, dc in next 2 dc, skip next dc, work FPtr around each of next 2 BPtr, dc in same BPtr just worked around and in next 2 dc, work FPtr around next BPtr, dc in last dc.

Row 15: Ch 3, turn; work BPtr around next FPtr, dc in next 4 sts, work BPtr around same FPtr just worked into and around next FPtr, skip next 2 dc, work BPtr around each of next 2 FPtr, dc in same FPtr just worked around and in next 3 dc, work BPtr around next FPtr, dc in last dc.

Row 16: Ch 3, turn; work FPtr around next BPtr, dc in next 4 dc, skip next 2 BPtr, work FPtr around each of next 2 BPtr, working **behind** 2 FPtr just made, work FPtr around first skipped BPtr and around next BPtr, dc in next 4 dc, work FPtr around next BPtr, dc in last dc.

Rows 17-113: Repeat Rows 3-16, 6 times, then repeat Rows 3-15 once **more**.
Finish off.

ASSEMBLY

Alternating Panels and beginning and ending with Panel A, lay out Panels with **right** sides facing and marked edges at bottom; sew Panels together *(Fig. 25, page 143)*.

EDGING

Rnd 1: With **right** side facing, join yarn with sc in any st; sc evenly around entire Afghan working 3 sc in each corner and working an even number of sc; join with slip st to first sc.

Rnd 2: Ch 3, do **not** turn; working from **left** to **right**, skip next sc, ★ work reverse hdc in next sc *(Figs. 19a-d, page 142)*, ch 1, skip next sc; repeat from ★ around; join with slip st to st at base of beginning ch-3, finish off.

SANTA'S SPREAD Continued from page 128.

Last Row: With **right** side facing, join Natural with sc in first sc; work LDC, (sc in next 3 sc, work LDC) across to last sc, sc in last sc; finish off.

Using photo as a guide for placement and holding 7 strands of Natural yarn together, each 22" long, add fringe evenly across short edges of Afghan *(Figs. 27a & c, page 143)*.

RUBY LACE Continued from page 132.

EDGING

Rnd 1: Ch 1, turn; sc in first sc, work 156 sc evenly spaced across to last sc, 3 sc in last sc; work 201 sc evenly spaced across end of rows; 3 sc in free loop of first ch *(Fig. 21b, page 142)*, working around beginning ch, work 156 sc evenly spaced across to marked ch, 3 sc in marked ch; work 201 sc evenly spaced across end of rows, 2 sc in same st as first sc; join with slip st to first sc: 726 sc.

Rnd 2: Slip st in next sc, ch 3, 4 dc in same st, (skip next 4 sc, 5 dc in next sc) across to next corner 3-sc group, skip corner 3-sc group, ★ 5 dc in next sc, (skip next 4 sc, 5 dc in next sc) across to next corner 3-sc group, skip corner 3-sc group; repeat from ★ 2 times **more**; join with slip st to top of beginning ch-3, finish off.

Holding 6 strands of yarn together, each 16" long, add fringe in each sp between 5-dc groups on short edges of Afghan *(Figs. 27a & c, page 143)*.

general instructions

BASIC INFORMATION

ABBREVIATIONS

BPdc	Back Post double crochet(s)
BPtr	Back Post treble crochet(s)
ch(s)	chain(s)
dc	double crochet(s)
Dk	Dark
dtr	double treble crochet(s)
FP	Front Post
FPdc	Front Post double crochet(s)
FPtr	Front Post treble crochet(s)
hdc	half double crochet(s)
LDC	Long double crochet(s)
LSC	Long single crochet(s)
Lt	Light
mm	millimeters
Rnd(s)	Round(s)
sc	single crochet(s)
sp(s)	space(s)
st(s)	stitch(es)
tr	treble crochet(s)
YO	yarn over

SYMBOLS

★ — work instructions following ★ as many **more** times as indicated in addition to the first time.

† to † or ♥ to ♥ — work all instructions from first † to second † or from first ♥ to second ♥ **as many** times as specified.

( ) or [ ] — work enclosed instructions **as many** times as specified by the number immediately following **or** work all enclosed instructions in the stitch or space indicated **or** contains explanatory remarks.

colon (:) — the number(s) given after a colon at the end of a row or round denote(s) the number of stitches you should have on that row or round.

TERMS

chain loosely — work the chain **only** loose enough for the hook to pass through the chain easily when working the next row or round into the chain.

post — the vertical shaft of a stitch.

right side vs. wrong side — the right side of your work is the side that will show when the piece is finished.

work across or around — continue working in the established pattern.

GAUGE

Gauge is the number of stitches and rows or rounds per inch and is used to determine the finished size of a project. All crochet patterns specify the gauge that you must match to ensure proper size and to ensure that you will have enough yarn to complete the project.

Hook size given in instructions is merely a guide. Because everyone crochets differently — loosely, tightly, or somewhere in between — the finished size can vary, even when crocheters use the very same pattern, yarn, and hook.

Before beginning any crocheted item, it is absolutely necessary for you to crochet a gauge swatch in the pattern stitch indicated and with the weight of yarn and hook size suggested. Your swatch must be large enough to measure your gauge. Lay your swatch on a hard, smooth, flat surface. Then measure it, counting your stitches and rows or rounds carefully. If your swatch is smaller than specified or you have too many stitches per inch, try again with a larger size hook; if your swatch is larger than specified or you don't have enough stitches per inch, try again with a smaller size hook. Keep trying until you find the size that will give you the specified gauge. DO NOT HESITATE TO CHANGE HOOK SIZE TO OBTAIN CORRECT GAUGE. Once proper gauge is obtained, measure width of piece approximately every 3" to be sure gauge remains consistent.

BASIC STITCH GUIDE

CHAIN *(abbreviated ch)*

To work a chain stitch, begin with a slip knot on the hook. Bring the yarn **over** hook from **back** to **front**, catching the yarn with the hook and turning the hook slightly toward you to keep the yarn from slipping off. Draw the yarn through the slip knot **(Fig. 1)**.

Fig. 1

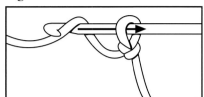

WORKING INTO THE CHAIN

When beginning a first row of crochet in a chain, always skip the first chain from the hook and work into the second chain from hook (for single crochet), third chain from hook (for half double crochet), or fourth chain from hook (for double crochet), etc. **(Fig. 2a)**.

Fig. 2a

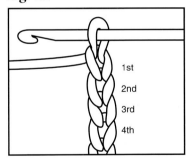

Method 1: Insert hook into back ridge of each chain indicated **(Fig. 2b)**.
Method 2: Insert hook under top loop **and** the back ridge of each chain indicated **(Fig. 2c)**.

Fig. 2b

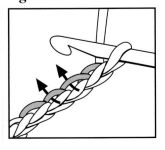

Fig. 2c

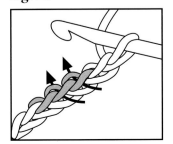

SLIP STITCH *(abbreviated slip st)*

This stitch is used to attach new yarn, to join work, or to move the yarn across a group of stitches without adding height. Insert hook in stitch or space indicated, YO and draw through stitch **and** loop on hook **(Fig. 3)**.

Fig. 3

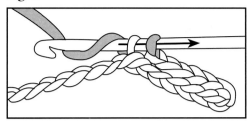

SINGLE CROCHET *(abbreviated sc)*

Insert hook in stitch or space indicated, YO and pull up a loop, YO and draw through both loops on hook **(Fig. 4)**.

Fig. 4

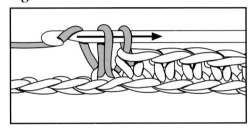

HALF DOUBLE CROCHET
(abbreviated hdc)

YO, insert hook in stitch or space indicated, YO and pull up a loop, YO and draw through all 3 loops on hook **(Fig. 5)**.

Fig. 5

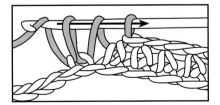

DOUBLE CROCHET (abbreviated dc)

YO, insert hook in stitch or space indicated, YO and pull up a loop (3 loops on hook), YO and draw through 2 loops on hook *(Fig. 6a)*, YO and draw through remaining 2 loops on hook *(Fig. 6b)*.

Fig. 6a

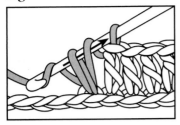

Fig. 6b

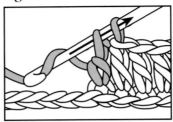

TREBLE CROCHET (abbreviated tr)

YO twice, insert hook in stitch or space indicated, YO and pull up a loop (4 loops on hook) *(Fig. 7a)*, (YO and draw through 2 loops on hook) 3 times *(Fig. 7b)*.

Fig. 7a

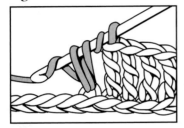

Fig. 7b

DOUBLE TREBLE CROCHET (abbreviated dtr)

YO 3 times, insert hook in stitch or space indicated, YO and pull up a loop (5 loops on hook) *(Fig. 8a)*, (YO and draw through 2 loops on hook) 4 times *(Fig. 8b)*.

Fig. 8a

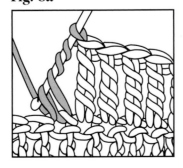

Fig. 8b

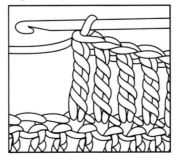

PATTERN STITCHES

LONG STITCH

Work single crochet (sc), or double crochet (dc), inserting hook in stitch or space indicated in instructions *(Fig. 9)*, and pulling up a loop even with loop on hook; complete stitch.

Fig. 9

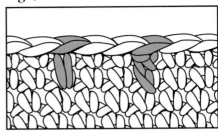

POST STITCH

Work around post of stitch indicated, inserting hook in direction of arrow *(Fig. 10)*.

Fig. 10

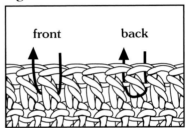

front   back

FRONT POST DOUBLE CROCHET (abbreviated FPdc)

YO, insert hook from **front** to **back** around post of stitch indicated *(Fig. 10)*, YO and pull up a loop (3 loops on hook) *(Fig. 11)*, (YO and draw through 2 loops on hook) twice.

Fig. 11

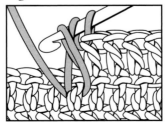

FRONT POST TREBLE CROCHET
(abbreviated FPtr)

YO twice, insert hook from **front** to **back** around post of stitch indicated *(Fig. 10)*, YO and pull up a loop (4 loops on hook) *(Fig. 12)*, (YO and draw through 2 loops on hook) 3 times.

Fig. 12

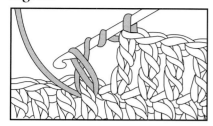

BACK POST DOUBLE CROCHET
(abbreviated BPdc)

YO, insert hook from **back** to **front** around post of stitch indicated *(Fig. 10)*, YO and pull up a loop (3 loops on hook) *(Fig. 13)*, (YO and draw through 2 loops on hook) twice.

Fig. 13

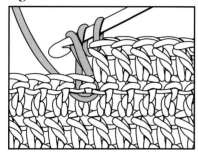

BACK POST TREBLE CROCHET
(abbreviated BPtr)

YO twice, insert hook from **back** to **front** around post of stitch indicated *(Fig. 10)*, YO and pull up a loop (4 loops on hook) *(Fig. 14)*, (YO and draw through 2 loops on hook) 3 times.

Fig. 14

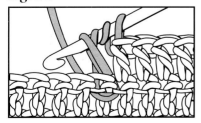

CLUSTER

A Cluster can be worked all in the same stitch or space *(Figs. 15a & b)*, **or** across several stitches *(Figs. 16a & b)*.

Fig. 15a

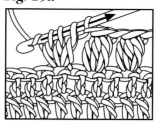

Fig. 15b

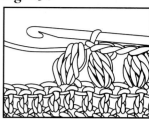

Fig. 16a

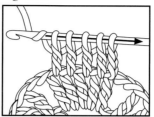

Fig. 16b

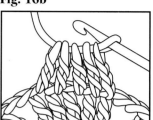

POPCORN

Work specified number of dc in stitch or space indicated, drop loop from hook, insert hook in first dc of dc group, hook dropped loop and draw through *(Fig. 17)*.

Fig. 17　　　**5-dc Popcorn**

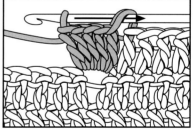

PUFF STITCH

★ YO, insert hook in stitch indicated, YO and pull up a loop even with loop on hook; repeat from ★ as many times as specified, YO and draw through all loops on hook *(Fig. 18)*.

Fig. 18

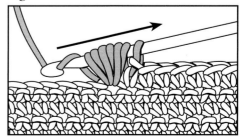

REVERSE HALF DOUBLE CROCHET
(abbreviated reverse hdc)

Working from **left** to **right**, YO, insert hook in st to right of hook *(Fig. 19a)*, YO and draw through, under, and to left of loop on hook (3 loops on hook) *(Fig. 19b)*, YO and draw through all 3 loops on hook *(Fig. 19c)* **(reverse hdc made, Fig. 219d)**.

Fig. 19a

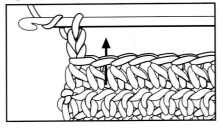

Fig. 19b

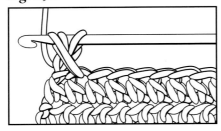

Fig. 19c

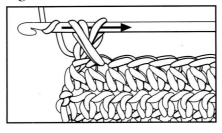

Fig. 19d

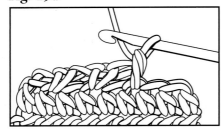

STITCHING TIPS

JOINING WITH SC

When instructed to join with sc, begin with a slip knot on hook. Insert hook in stitch or space indicated, YO and pull up a loop, YO and draw through both loops on hook.

BACK OR FRONT LOOP ONLY

Work only in loop(s) indicated by arrow *(Fig. 20)*.

Fig. 20

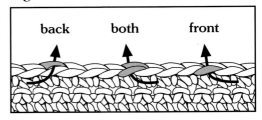

back   both   front

FREE LOOPS

After working in Back or Front Loops Only on a row or round, there will be a ridge of unused loops. These are called the free loops. Later, when instructed to work in the free loops of the same row or round, work in these loops *(Fig. 21a)*.
When instructed to work in a free loop of a beginning chain, work in loop indicated by arrow *(Fig. 21b)*.

Fig. 21a

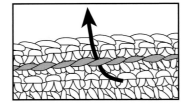

Fig. 21b

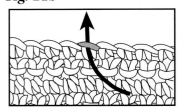

CHANGING COLORS

Work the last stitch to within one step of completion, hook new yarn *(Fig. 22a)* and draw through loops on hook. Cut old yarn and work over both ends unless otherwise specified.
When working in rounds or changing colors with a slip st, drop old yarn; using new yarn, join with slip stitch to first stitch *(Fig. 22b)*.

Fig. 22a

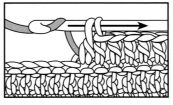

Fig. 22b

WORKING IN SPACE BEFORE STITCH

When instructed to work in space **before** a stitch or in spaces **between** stitches, insert hook in space indicated by arrow *(Fig. 23)*.

Fig. 23

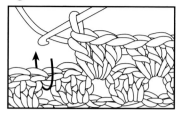

NO-SEW JOINING

Hold Squares, Motifs, or Strips with **wrong** sides together. Slip st or sc into sp as indicated *(Fig. 24)*.

Fig. 24

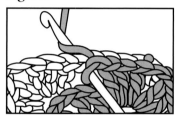

FINISHING

WEAVING SEAMS

With **right** side of two pieces facing you and edges even, sew through both pieces once to secure the beginning of the seam, leaving an ample yarn end to weave in later. Insert the needle from **right** to **left** through one strand on each piece *(Fig. 25)*. Bring the needle around and insert it from **right** to **left** through the next strand on both pieces. Continue in this manner, drawing seam together as you work.

Fig. 25

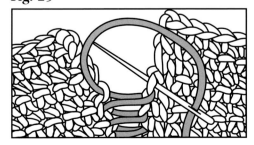

WHIPSTITCH

With **wrong** sides together and beginning in corner stitch, sew through both pieces once to secure the beginning of the seam, leaving an ample yarn end to weave in later. Insert needle from **front** to **back** through **inside** loops of **each** piece *(Fig. 26a)* **or** through **both** loops *(Fig. 26b)*. Bring needle around and insert it from **front** to **back** through the next loops of **both** pieces. Continue in this manner across to corner, keeping the sewing yarn fairly loose.

Fig. 26a   **Fig. 26b**

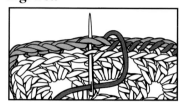   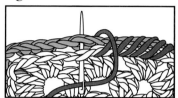

FRINGE

Cut a piece of cardboard 8" wide and ¹/₂" longer than desired fringe. Wind the yarn **loosely** and **evenly** around the length of the cardboard until the card is filled, then cut across one end; repeat as needed. Align the number of strands desired and fold in half.

With **wrong** side facing and using a crochet hook, draw the folded end up through a stitch, row, or loop, and pull the loose ends through the folded end *(Figs. 27a & b)*; draw the knot up **tightly** *(Figs. 27c & d)*. Repeat, spacing as specified. Lay flat on a hard surface and trim the ends.

Fig. 27a   **Fig. 27b**

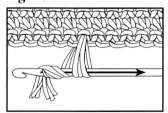   

Fig. 27c   **Fig. 27d**

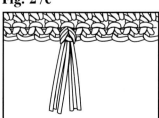   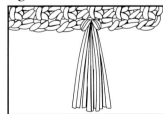

credits

To Magna IV Color Imaging of Little Rock, Arkansas, we say thank you for the superb color reproduction and excellent pre-press preparation.

We want to especially thank photographers Ken West, Larry Pennington, Mark Mathews, and Karen Shirey of Peerless Photography, Little Rock, Arkansas, and Jerry R. Davis of Jerry Davis Photography, Little Rock, Arkansas, for their time, patience, and excellent work.

We would like to extend a special word of thanks to the talented designers who created the lovely projects in this book:

Carol Alexander: *Serene Wrap*, page 110
Carol Alexander and Brenda Stratton: *Rosy Wrap*, page 68
Mary Lamb Becker: *Cuddly Snowballs*, page 8; *Harvest Gold*, page 116
Joan Beebe: *Seashell Illusion*, page 84
Jennie Black: *Grandmother's Garden*, page 42
Nair Carswell: *Garden Romance*, page 62
Patricia Pattenotte Eudy: *Ivory Elegance*, page 98
Nancy Fuller: *Brilliant Contrast*, page 92
Anne Halliday: *Chill Chaser*, page 6; *Serene Granny*, page 10; *Country Hearts*, page 22; *Dreamy Flowers*, page 44; *Flowers for Baby*, page 52; *Spider Lace*, page 54; *Seaside Dreams*, page 78; *Quiet Comfort*, page 80; *Pebble Beach*, page 88; *Ebb and Flow*, page 90; *Playtime Granny*, page 104; *Winter White*, page 122; *Soothing Ripples*, page 124
Terry Kimbrough: *Cuddly Valentine*, page 18; *Field of Daisies*, page 70; *Emerald Treasure*, page 130
Valesha Marshell Kirksey: *Spring Days*, page 28
Jennine Korejko: *Lovely in Lavender*, page 40
Tammy Kreimeyer: *Hearts & Lace*, page 20; *Budding Beauty*, page 32; *Engaging Pattern*, page 56
Melissa Leapman: *Bed of Roses*, page 16; *Teardrop Garden*, page 38; *Climbing Vines*, page 96; *Pleasing Plaid*, page 100; *Marvelous Mosaic*, page 108; *Distinctive Design*, page 120; *Santa's Spread*, page 128
Sarah Anne Phillips: *Windowpane Wrap*, page 86
Carole Prior: *Welcome, Baby!* page 30; *Summer Style*, page 66; *Sapphire Sea*, page 102; *Colorful Coverlet*, page 112; *Ruby Lace*, page 132
Katherine Satterfield: *Posy Patch Wrap*, page 34; *Mile-A-Minute Violets*, page 58
Ruth Shepherd: *Graceful Shells*, page 64
Mary Ann Sipes: *May Jewels*, page 50
Martha Brooks Stein: *Dutch Rose*, page 114
Brenda E. Stratton for Alexander-Stratton Designs, Inc.: *Beautiful Braids*, page 12
Carole Rutter Tippet: *Appealing Aran*, page 134
Julene S. Watson: *Country Warmer*, page 126